Barnes & Noble Shakespeare

David Scott Kastan
Series Editor

BARNES & NOBLE SHAKESPEARE features newly edited texts of the plays prepared by the world's premiere Shakespeare scholars. Each edition provides new scholarship with an introduction, commentary, unusually full and informative notes, an account of the play as it would have been performed in Shakespeare's theaters, and an essay on how to read Shakespeare's language.

DAVID SCOTT KASTAN is the Old Dominion Foundation Professor in the Humanities at Columbia University and one of the world's leading authorities on Shakespeare.

Barnes & Noble Shakespeare
Published by Barnes & Noble
122 Fifth Avenue
New York, NY 10011
www.barnesandnoble.com/shakespeare

© 2007 Barnes & Noble, Inc.

Image on p. 290:
William Shakespeare, *Comedies, Histories, & Tragedies*, London, 1623, Bequest of Stephen Whitney Phoenix, Rare Book & Manuscript Library, Columbia University.

Library of Congress Cataloging-in-Publication Data

Shakespeare, William, 1564–1616
  Twelfth Night / [William Shakespeare].
    p. cm. — (Barnes & Noble Shakespeare)
  Includes bibliographical references.
  ISBN-13: 978-1-4114-0118-1 (alk. paper)
  ISBN-10: 1-4114-0118-2 (alk. paper)
  1. Survival after airplane accidents, shipwrecks, etc.—Drama. 2. Brothers and sisters—Drama. 3. Mistaken identity—Drama. 4. Illyria—Drama. 5. Twins—Drama. I. Title. II. Series: Shakespeare, William, 1564–1616. Works. 2006.

PR2837.A1 2006
822.3'3—dc22   2006009486

Printed and bound in the United States.
    20 19

TWELFTH NIGHT

William

SHAKESPEARE

CLAIRE MCEACHERN

EDITOR

Barnes & Noble Shakespeare

Contents

Introduction to *Twelfth Night*
by Claire McEachern

A playgoer in Shakespeare's time who attended a performance of *Twelfth Night* would have encountered, much as we do, a play whose plot turns on the pleasurable mistakes into which love can lead a person. Viola, a plucky young woman, shipwrecked and separated from her twin brother and cast ashore in a strange country, disguises herself as a young man in order to enter the service of the local duke. The duke employs this page as an emissary to the woman he loves, a woman who has sworn not to love but rather to mourn her own recently dead brother. However, confronted with the impassioned pleas of the emissary, who has fallen in love with her master and thus knows whereof she speaks when it comes to the pangs of love, the disdainful woman falls in love with Viola (now named Cesario) and enters into her own plight of unrequited passion. This impasse is unknotted only by the arrival of the twin brother, who happily marries the lady and brings to light the true gender identity of his sister. The duke then considers marriage to his page, whose devotions he has oft heard sworn. The nominal themes of the play are, then, the questions of why and how and whom people love and how they respond to the experience of longing.

Unlike us, however, this playgoer may have sensed some connection between the play's obvious romantic concerns and other, more supernatural, mysteries. These were mysteries brought into being by the most profound cultural change of the sixteenth century, that from Catholicism to Protestantism in England's national religion. Perhaps most pressing among the reverberations of this shift were not ideological or political questions, but practical and emotional ones: how was God to be worshipped, how were sins to be acknowledged and remedied, and how was salvation itself to be hoped for? These questions, and the emotions they summon, resonate with the errant longings dramatized in Shakespeare's comedy.

For instance, whether in thinking about the history of the world, or the history of their own lives, sixteenth-century believers would, like *Twelfth Night*'s characters, have confronted a story in which a temporary confusion about identity was resolved by revelation of truth. The Christian history of the world had always been framed as a period of earthly confusion and error set to rights by the Last Judgment, the moment when all true values are determined—when the meek, for example, however heretofore underestimated, might inherit the earth. The individual experienced this confusion as a mystery concerning his or her own salvation and ultimate destination (Heaven or Hell?), a mystery sustained throughout the individual's lifetime and resolved only, presumably, after his or her death. This Christian story urged that the material world, where what usually mattered was the satisfaction of one's carnal desires, might not be an accurate guide to the celestial system of measuring value. Success on earth might count against you in Heaven, whereas earthly misery might prepare the way for heavenly bliss.

The introduction of Protestantism in the sixteenth century increased the extent of mystery in this story. Under Catholicism, salvation had been a matter of following certain clear rules, such as doing good works and making sure spiritual debts were paid and absolved and truly repented at the moment of death—hence confession, pardons, and other protocols of spiritual laundering. When Protestants abolished such practices and developed a theology of salvation based solely on the gift of God's grace to the sinner—in other words, not based on the sinner's own efforts—it became harder to measure how one was faring, salvation-wise. A person who took his or her salvation seriously at this time was in for a potentially rather anxious experience. For instance, was worldly fortune such as material prosperity or success in romance a sign that God had favored you, a sampling of delights to come in the afterworld? Or was it a sign that you kept company with earthly temptations and were hence damned? Were difficulties marks of disfavor or opportunities to show your spiritual mettle? How was a person to interpret the world around her as a guide to her spiritual destiny? How could one judge the fitness of one's own desires, whether for earthly or heavenly rewards? Should one hope? Fear? Trust? Suspect?

Theologians of the period were divided not only on how a person could know whether he or she was destined for Heaven, but whether it was appropriate even to ask. The influential French reformer Jean Calvin, for instance, thought it essentially impudent to attempt to ascertain God's plan for you, while the English theologian Richard Hooker thought that if you were worried about whether you were saved, then chances are you probably were: anxiety itself was a good sign, doubt giving you benefit of the doubt. The only consensus was pretty much that either extreme—utter confidence in one's own election, or utter despair about it—was a bad idea. The one led to a dangerous smugness or elitism, the other led to disregard for law and order.

This is the world of _Twelfth Night_, a play that offers characters at sea with the mysterious signs of the world and asks what the proper attitude is toward our own longings for rewards. Some of its resonances with these matters are quite specific. We can, for instance, find representatives of both categories of spiritual error, in the two antagonists of the play's subplot, Malvolio the presumptious steward, and Sir Toby Belch, his chief antagonist and tormenter. The one is called a "kind of puritan," *puritan* being a blanket term in this period for religious extremists dissatisfied with what they considered the insufficiently reformed state of the national church and more than usually convinced of their own ethical worth. The unruly knight, on the other hand, is seemingly concerned only with physical pleasures, "cakes and ale." Malvolio's opinion of himself is too high, while Sir Toby seems insufficiently preoccupied with gratifications beyond the immediate. While this play sets these two figures at odds with each other, in English social life both Puritans and libertines were equally disruptive, in that neither respected the orders and hierarchies, based in caste, that dictated that the socially noble were also the ethically noble.

However, we needn't be so specific or even so serious in our search for this play's cultural resonances. *Twelfth Night* is not explicitly a religious play, and it is a play that cautions against reading into things, but it is at the very least a play that foregrounds the experience of longing and the nature of its objects, reasons, and mistakes. The universe of the play is overrun by errant desires founded on mistaken identities. The most far-reaching of these stems from a disguise, that of the heroine Viola as a boy. As in Shakespeare's source, Barnaby Riche's "Apolonius and Silla" (1581), this disguise is a practical one, both protective and liberating. Yet in Illyria, Viola stumbles into a world awry at the highest levels, where errors deriving from psychological misconceptions precede and prepare for those caused by her disguise. For instance, the most desirable heiress, Olivia, refuses to return the attentions of the most desirable bachelor, Orsino, a stalemate that offers itself as the obstacle this comedy must overcome. Furthermore, Olivia has sworn to mourn her recently dead brother for seven years.

Compounding her perversity is the fact that she rules only tenuously over her household. The only male authority figure is her drunken uncle, himself largely keen on using her status as a wealthy heiress to fleece potential suitors of their money to serve his own appetites. Even her deceased father's fool cannot be kept to heel.

Viola's arrival only compounds and further confounds the state of misdirected longings that exists between Orsino and Olivia, and to this trio of confused lovers we can add Malvolio, the sea captain Antonio, Sir Toby, and even Sir Andrew Aguecheek. Malvolio is duped into thinking his mistress Olivia wishes him to make love to her. Antonio, in love with the twin brother Sebastian, is led by Cesario's failure to recognize him, which he interprets as a refusal to acknowledge him, into thinking his affections even more unrequited than they probably are. Sir Toby is usually too drunk to recognize that the maidservant Maria carries a torch for him, and even Sir Andrew, egged on by Sir Toby, briefly thinks he has a shot at Olivia. (It is the latter's only redeeming quality that he has enough sense to realize he's not in the running).

But errors about whom one loves and who loves one back are not the only kind of errors in this play. Viola is obviously exempt from the erotic errors due to her disguise. She, along with the audience, is mostly in the privileged position of realizing the mistakes of others, and she alone seems humbly unambitious in accepting that her love for Orsino will go both unrequited and largely unspoken. But even Viola is not exempt from the general climate of "midsummer madness." For instance, she is led astray about the alleged swordsmanship of Sir Andrew, as he is about hers—a mistake about manhood, at least. She is further nonplussed by Antonio's mistaking her for her brother, and on a more serious level, she is wrong about the alleged death of her brother, as Sebastian is about hers. So, too, the fool Feste points out to his mistress Olivia that she is wrong to mourn her own truly dead brother, who, if in Heaven rather than Hell or this vale of tears, ought to be the object of celebration. The response to earthly loss and the consequent misunderstanding of providence is perhaps the most fundamental and metaphysical error that the play addresses. But even Feste, who seems to intuit something fishy about Viola's disguise and usually possesses the poised gaze of the outside observer, is flummoxed by Sebastian's arrival on the scene into the same condition of confusion as everyone else: "Nothing that is so is so." Pretty much the only characters in _Twelfth Night_ who don't labor under some delusion are the servants Maria and Fabian.

Characters are mistaken about themselves as well as others—in fact, mistakes about others usually begin at home. Olivia first asserts that she is immune to love, and then that she can make Cesario love her, even if it means bribing him. Orsino, just as willful, is convinced he will prevail in his suit and sends jewels to Olivia in the service of that cause. Antonio's otherwise enigmatic insistence that Sebastian take his purse falls into the same category of gifts. The self-absorbed desire of a lover to elbow his way past obstacles also describes Malvolio. Indeed, while Olivia accuses Malvolio of being "sick of self-love," the description fits many of the characters as well— except, strikingly, Viola, who as a twin is in a position to know that selves are not necessarily so special. Paradoxically, however, hers is the most original voice in the play, in terms of the poetry Shakespeare writes for her. Self-love, and its corollary conviction that other people can and should share your affliction, seems a nearly universal illness and contributes a great deal to the hallucinatory world in which these characters find themselves. Twinship is thus not only a biological fact in this play but also a metaphor for the way in which we all have in common a self often blindly insistent on the furtherance of its own will.

For the most part, Shakespeare seems to argue for a lenient take on longing: we can be misguided and inappropriate in our pursuit of our wills, but not, for the most part, any more so than the next person, and ultimately providence will do its best to set us straight (literally, in the case of Olivia). Take, for example, the difference between Viola and Olivia's respective responses to loss. Both women have lost brothers, in another instance of human twinship. Viola, for instance, knows her brother may well be dead but does not allow the knowledge to prevent her from choosing life. In fact, she extrapolates the possibility of his survival from her own and allows herself to choose love despite the possibility of further loss or even lack of reciprocity. Her resilience could appear as heartless or even fickle, or even imprudent in its disregard for the temporary nature of earthly happiness—except it doesn't, for she seems, fittingly, buoyant. Of course, the experience of love she embarks on is hardly without its elements of loss, or even of self-protection: she loves a man in love with another woman, who doesn't even know that she, Viola, is a woman. But it is her doubly hopeless experience of love that renders her love-language alone authentic. Hers is an exorbitant yearning that sunders the conventions of Petrarchan desire—the trite set "text" of Orsino's bosom—through the sheer force of her passion. Much as Olivia is drawn despite her vows to Viola/Cesario's sincerity, so Viola is the audience's touchstone of truth as well, the protagonist with whom we are most asked to identify. We the audience always know who she is, even more so than she does, in that as of Act Two, scene one, we know her brother to be alive, and hence that her psychological buoyancy is warranted and just, not impertinent but rather full of faith.

Olivia, by contrast, under the double burden of the recent losses of both father and brother, initially appears unwilling to risk any further casualties, the kind that loving might involve. While this disregard for earthly delights might seem an instance of spiritual good posture, it also demonstrates a kind of presumptuous contempt for both the world's bounties and its necessities. She is, in essence, impolite. Orsino in fact calls her "you uncivil lady." Especially as it is not a very sincere abstinence; the greed with which she pursues and falls on Cesario/Sebastian reveals her merely as a familiar comic type, the disdainer of love forced to recant. But to the extent that her fruitless pining serves to correct and balance her previous disdain, we allow her to pass relatively uncensored. Olivia's final cry of "Most wonderful!" at the sight of two husbands at once seems to bespeak a nature duly apprised of a sense of the world's bounty.

Both of these love experiences offer instances of a kind of chastisement, of characters being made to suffer for love before being rewarded with it. Adding to their rebuke is the fact that the characters' rewards are not precisely the ones they had imagined for themselves. Most of the play's other lovers are also forgivable, probably because they too are humbled in the course of the plot, forced to renounce their own willfulness and self-love.

Orsino's desire for Olivia, for instance, is arrogant and formulaic. We are told (by Olivia no less) that he is eminently attractive. But he also knows it. He in love with the love lifestyle, convinced that she will love him eventually, certain that he knows everything there is to know about women, that female longing is inferior to male, and that he cannot and will not countenance Olivia's rejection of his suit. He is wrong about all of this, and hence Olivia's insistent refusals are quite satisfying to us. In Viola he gets more than he deserves, but we're willing to give him that, probably because for Viola's sake we give him the benefit of the doubt (like those couples where one partner's appeal legislates for the elusive redeeming qualities of the other). Besides, when it comes to love, who doesn't get more than they deserve? To these three humiliations we can add Antonio's; his deflected love for Sebastian is truly pathetic and literally life threatening (much like Viola's, actually, in one of the play's many twinships of the spirit), and he of these four is the only one who does not ultimately gain some consolation prize, apart from his life. The others all get something extra, even if it is not who they expected. Such is the imprecise if well-meaning bounty of comic providence, whose grace often consists in delivering not what you think you want but what you might not know you need.

The play's treatment of stubborn and self-involved lovers is, then, largely a forgiving and even festive one. Shakespeare makes this festive quality quite explicit in the play's title. In Renaissance Europe, the twelfth night of the Christmas holiday season fell on January 6th, the feast of the Epiphany. This day celebrated the moment in the Christmas story when the three wise men arrive to present their gifts to the infant Christ. It was a day both of revelation and of restoration, commemorating the moment when Christ's birth was fully revealed to the entirety of the world, and his status as the one true lord recognized by the homage of temporal rulers. Like the pagan celebrations of the winter solstice onto which the Christian calendar grafted its own winter festivities, the Epiphany marked the paradoxical presence of light amid darkness. The calendrical twin of *Twelfth Night* is Shakespeare's play of the summer solstice, *A Midsummer Night's Dream*.

The people of Shakespeare's England celebrated Twelfth Night with games, masquerades, entertainments, and indeed plays. Often, the normal social rules governing rank and gender were temporarily suspended during these activities. In fact, while *Twelfth Night* was first printed in the 1623 First Folio of Shakespeare's plays, it was probably written in 1600 or 1601, for one of the earliest records of its performance comes from a contemporary report of a young lawyer named John Manningham, who saw the play performed during the midwinter feast of Candlemas in 1602 in the banqueting hall of the Middle Temple (a London law school). Candlemas was a holiday forty days after Christmas, one of the last feasts of the winter holiday season prior to the arrival of Lenten abstinence. The feast of the Epiphany was in effect a rehearsal for the revelations and recognitions of Easter, even as Easter was itself a model for the end of days. *Twelfth Night* thus both mimicked and leavened the larger Christian story. Anyone might be king for a day during holiday time, but only Christ was king when it was over.

The holiday games of the Christmas feast season help shed light on the festival tones of Shakespeare's play. Indeed, the event of the Epiphany models the process of the plot: the confusions caused by Viola's disguise are unknotted by the arrival of the real thing—in this case, not Christ but Sebastian. But Sebastian's arrival does not fix Malvolio's problem, even as Malvolio's problem is not caused by Viola's disguise. If *Twelfth Night* largely proposes a light rather than anxious view of the ways in which the world and our own longings for happiness can mislead us, in this exception to the general festive rule Shakespeare asks us to evaluate the nature of our longing more somberly.

Not all love delusions are created equal in this play. While most entertain, Malviolio's usually disgusts, or at the least makes us uncomfortable (much depends here on a particular performance's choices). He is not included in the harmonious couplings of the ending; indeed, he presents a conspicuous obstacle to their resolution. Interestingly, the only element of the play's plot noted in Manningham's record of the 1602 Candlemas performance concerns Malvolio's plight, as if it alone stood out in his memory: "A good practice in it to make the Steward believe his Lady Widdow was in love with him." In Malvolio's ungainly experience of love, the play asks us to ponder the difference between a love delusion that is merely silly or even endearing, and one that is grotesque. Olivia's love for Cesario/Viola, for instance, is funny and slightly risqué; Orsino's for Olivia is fashionable but harmless enough; Viola's for Orsino perhaps a bit perplexing, given what we know of her and she of him; Antonio's for Sebastian is helplessly self-sacrificing. But Malvolio's love for Olivia is ridiculous and verges on the repugnant.

Our reaction to Malvolio cannot merely be a matter of our distaste for social climbing—a distaste that the play gives voice to in Olivia's own reluctance to wed above her station. For we are meant, I think, to cheer on Maria's match to Sir Toby as a Cinderella story, a parable of wit rewarded with social elevation—the same goes for Viola and Orsino. One category of longing (that of Olivia, Orsino, Viola, and Antonio) represents an error we perhaps share and forgive, but the other is one we would disown—our response to the one is sheepish, the other, shameful. This double response demonstrates Shakespeare's indebtedness in *Twelfth Night* to two kinds of comedy, one inclusive in its mockery (the kind we laugh with), and the kind that is satirical and scapegoating (the kind we laugh at). Scholars of *Twelfth Night* have in fact been long divided as to whether the play represents Shakespeare at the peak of his frivolous best, or heading mordantly toward the problem comedies such as *All's Well That Ends Well* and *Measure for Measure*.

In many respects, Malvolio's love longing fits the same profile as the others. It is no more willful than Olivia's or Orsino's. It is no more hopeless than Antonio's, and like Olivia or Viola, Malvolio loves somebody in love with somebody else (the overlapping spellings of their names enforces the comparison). It is an instance of seeking to love above his station, and Olivia's punctiliousness on this score perhaps sets a certain standard of decorum. But in that case Viola's love for Orsino is an overreaching one, since if the Duke Orsino is too high for the countess Olivia, he is for the mere gentlewoman Viola as well. So we cannot account for Malvolio's lack of appeal in those terms alone.

It is also difficult to charge him on other counts. There is something unsavory in Malvolio's alphabetical speculations on Olivia's genitals and "great P's," but, to be fair, so is there in Orsino's musings on Cesario's pipe and lips, although the latter is admittedly less scatological or urological. Malvolio is a hypocrite—a spoilsport of others' pleasures who nonetheless cannot refrain from entertaining his own fantasies of sensual indulgence. His very name means "ill will." Even more damning, he is a stander upon ceremony who hopes to overleap it by marrying his mistress. But if he is a hypocrite, so, in some sense, is his mistress. Even Olivia's exorbitant mourning has a kind of hedonism to it—she plans to luxuriate in it.

On these scores, Malvolio seems fairly typical of the play's lovers and indeed of most human beings: somewhat self-absorbed, somewhat self-deceived, prey to the desire to love and be loved in return. Why then is his chastisement so much more severe than theirs? Why does Malvolio alone suffer the humiliation of the dark house scene and the imputation that he is mad—the true indignity for a man who prides himself on his self-control? Wouldn't the humiliation of error, having worn yellow cross-garters, and incessant smiling be enough, if added to the knowledge that his beloved—for whom he has done things so grossly out of character—does not love him in return, indeed, barely considers him a sexual being? Most of us at one time or another love somebody who doesn't love us back, making fools of ourselves in the process, but that ought to argue for our sympathy with this character, not our disdain. Instead we feel shame, both at the spectacle of his desire and then at the scene of his humiliation. Indeed, one of the confusing things about the figure of Malvolio is that while we want to see him punished, the punishment itself makes us squirm.

Something separates Malvolio's longing from those of the other characters. Part of it is his certainty about his goals; Maria's forged letter plays upon preexisting daydreams about Olivia's favor. The nakedness and presumption of his hopes are the first source of our discomfort, and even more damning is the fact that once encouraged, he does not have the grace to admit doubt or failure. In this he is so unlike Viola, but not that different from Olivia or Orsino. This confidence is what is most unsettling, and puritanical in the religious sense. Malvolio is not so much a killjoy (though he is that, too) as someone convinced without a doubt, unwilling to acknowledge the provisional quality of rewards or his own desert, and certain he is better than others, or that he will be soon enough. So part of what galls about Malvolio, and what we, too, want to see punished, is his utter conviction of his own rightness—he is "a kind of puritan" in his certainty of his own worth, that he will get what he deserves and deserve what he gets. These are dangerous premises in human loving, Christian salvation, and social mobility alike. But again, not necessarily atypical assumptions for any human.

A more compelling reason for his lack of appeal may lie in the nature of the object for which he longs. His erotic daydreams are not so much about sex but about power and have mostly to do with the political degradation of others. It is not so much Olivia's soul or even body that he desires but her social position. In his sex fantasy, he leaves her sleeping in a daybed (only aristocrats get to go to bed in the daytime) in order to lecture her uncle about his behavior, so that the climax of Malvolio's erotic fantasy is not his own ejaculation but Sir Toby's curtsy. It galls him sorely that people better born do not need to behave as well as he does—a self-made man who can't afford to misbehave, he chafes against his own subordination to persons "lighter" in comportment if heavier in social worth. While we may sympathize with his subjection, it is not clear he would do so were the positions reversed. Malvolio's erotic ambitions are part Cinderella story, part revenge fantasy.

Again, social ambition is not unique to Malvolio; Maria has herself apparently been practicing Olivia's handwriting. But what is unique to him, and what the incongruity of the Cinderella metaphor brings forth, is the peculiar role gender plays in Malvolio's attempts at social elevation, and how its presence reveals the terrible, even terrifying dependency of his position. If Malvolio were to marry up, he would be a man who owed his new position to a woman. Viola and Maria both marry up in this play, but we are used to thinking of women as socially dependent. Men so dependent appear in a significantly different light. The humiliating and emasculating nature of Malvolio's situation was not an unfamiliar position for male courtiers of Elizabeth I, themselves subordinate to and dependent on a powerful, socially superior female. This play seems to propose a tolerant shrug—"what you will"—when it comes to the gender assignments of most couplings (boy and boy, girl and girl, boy and girl, whatever you please), and a similar leniency is extended to the case of a man marrying beneath himself (Sir Toby, Orsino). But Malvolio's situation forces us to confront the fact that anything does not go when it comes to all possible combinations of social ranks and gender roles. Theologically speaking, dependency was the correct relation of the helpless soul to the selective generosity of a Protestant God. However, the radically feminine nature of this dependency made it an uncomfortable posture to assume, as the Holy Sonnets of the poet John Donne make clear. The vulnerability of Malvolio's longing is one we'd do anything to avoid acknowledging, or sharing.

Thus what Malvolio's case forces us to realize is that we, too, are snobs. Even worse, we are sexist snobs. In consenting to the comic resolution offered by this play, one which excludes him, we must confront our own desires for exclusivity, and the way in which being chosen, even if it's to be a member of a big and relatively inclusive group (suitably chastised well-born romantic lovers of heterosexual objects), means that some people must also be excluded from that group, otherwise the category of the chosen has no meaning. The Chorus to Shakespeare's *Henry V* addresses the audience as "gentles all"; if *Twelfth Night* had a chorus, it would more likely speak to "gentles only." Malvolio is a scapegoat, someone required to bear the sins of the community. Unlike some scapegoats, however, he is one who refuses to go quietly and who hence shames us with our own need for a scapegoat, who makes us confront our own elitism and the limits of our own comic tolerance.

Twelfth Night ends oddly for a comedy. While as a meditation on the common and comic failings of human nature it is often profound, it is not a play that strives to establish much psychic specificity in its characters, and hence it foregoes a sense of deep compatibility in its romantic pairings. Even by Shakespeare's standards, there is a fair degree of arbitrariness to the final couplings. Some historians have argued that the play demonstrates the early modern sense that the differences between men and women were a matter of degree rather than opposition. Others have argued that it demonstrates the Renaissance conviction that gender identity was established purely at the level of social signs—that clothes alone can make the man (or woman). But while Orsino may segue easily enough from homoerotic affection to heterosexual union, Olivia, who thinks she is marrying the eloquent and effacing speaker of the willow-cabin lament, has in fact betrothed herself to a swordsman capable of bloodying the brow of her kinsman, who conspicuously lacks the humility of his twin sister when it comes to a conviction of his own lovability. Sebastian takes Olivia's love for him for granted much in the same way he does Antonio's. There is something brutal here.

Other contradictions of comic harmony persist. Viola's "womans weeds" are still held hostage, in the possession of her sea captain—himself mysteriously imprisoned by a Malvolio not likely to be mollified anytime soon, absent an ability to laugh at himself. Antonio is, we hope, going to be allowed to live, if not as part of the nuptial congress. The most authentic emotional resolution of the play lies less with the union of sexual partners than the awkward reunion of siblings; for while both kinds of union work to defeat death, the death defeated by the return of a lost sibling, who in turn recalls and repairs the death of a parent, is the death less capable of being redressed through procreation. Shakespeare may satisfy comic form and expectations here, but he does so mockingly, almost with a kind of contempt, giving us "what we will," but forcing us to acknowledge the stubbornness of our desire for tidy endings and what we are willing to sacrifice for them.

Shakespeare and His England
by David Scott Kastan

S hakespeare is a household name, one of those few that don't need a first name to be instantly recognized. His first name was, of course, William, and he (and it, in its Latin form, *Gulielmus*) first came to public notice on April 26, 1564, when his baptism was recorded in the parish church of Stratford-upon-Avon, a small market town about ninety miles northwest of London. It isn't known exactly when he was born, although traditionally his birthday is taken to be April 23rd. It is a convenient date (perhaps too convenient) because that was the date of his death in 1616, as well as the date of St. George's Day, the annual feast day of England's patron saint. It is possible Shakespeare was born on the 23rd; no doubt he was born within a day or two of that date. In a time of high rates of infant mortality, parents would not wait long after a baby's birth for the baptism. Twenty percent of all children would die before their first birthday.

Life in 1564, not just for infants, was conspicuously vulnerable. If one lived to age fifteen, one was likely to live into one's fifties, but probably no more than 60 percent of those born lived past their mid-teens. Whole towns could be ravaged by epidemic disease. In 1563, the year before Shakespeare was born, an outbreak of plague claimed over one third of the population of London. Fire, too, was a constant threat; the thatched roofs of many houses were highly flammable, as well as offering handy nesting places for insects and rats. Serious crop failures in several years of the decade of the 1560s created food short-ages, severe enough in many cases to lead to the starvation of the elderly and the infirm, and lowering the resistances of many others so that between 1536 and 1560 influenza claimed over 200,000 lives.

Shakespeare's own family in many ways reflected these unsettling realities. He was one of eight children, two of whom did not survive their first year, one of whom died at age eight; one lived to twenty-seven, while the four surviving siblings died at ages ranging from Edmund's thirty-nine to William's own fifty-two years. William married at an unusually early age. He was only eighteen, though his wife was twenty-six, almost exactly the norm of the day for women, though men normally married also in their mid- to late twenties. Shakespeare's wife Anne was already pregnant at the time that the marriage was formally confirmed, and a daughter, Susanna, was born six months later, in May 1583. Two years later, she gave birth to twins, Hamnet and Judith. Hamnet would die in his eleventh year.

If life was always at risk from what Shakespeare would later call "the thousand natural shocks / That flesh is heir to" (*Hamlet*, 3.1.61–62), the incessant threats to peace were no less unnerving, if usually less immediately life threatening. There were almost daily rumors of foreign invasion and civil war as the Protestant Queen Eliz-abeth assumed the crown in 1558 upon the death of her Catholic half sister, Mary. Mary's reign had been marked by the public burnings of Protestant "heretics," by the seeming subordination of England to Spain, and by a commitment to a ruinous war with France, that, among its other effects, fueled inflation and encouraged a debasing of the currency. If, for many, Elizabeth represented the hopes for a peaceful and prosperous Protestant future, it seemed unlikely in the early days of her rule that the young monarch could hold her England together against the twin menace of the powerful Catholic monarchies of Europe and the significant part of her own population who were reluctant to give up their old faith. No wonder the Queen's principal secretary saw England in the early years of Elizabeth's rule as a land surrounded by "perils many, great and imminent."

In Stratford-upon-Avon, it might often have been easy to forget what threatened from without. The simple rural life, shared by about 90 percent of the English populace, had its reassuring natural rhythms and delights. Life was structured by the daily rising and setting of the sun, and by the change of seasons. Crops were planted and harvested; livestock was bred, its young delivered; sheep were sheared, some livestock slaughtered. Market days and fairs saw the produce and crafts of the town arrayed as people came to sell and shop—and be entertained by musicians, dancers, and troupes of actors. But even in Stratford, the lurking tensions and dangers could be daily sensed. A few months before Shakespeare was born, there had been a shocking "defacing" of images in the church, as workmen, not content merely to whitewash over the religious paintings decorating the interior as they were ordered, gouged large holes in those felt to be too "Catholic"; a few months after Shakespeare's birth, the register of the same church records another deadly outbreak of plague. The sleepy market town on the northern bank of the gently flowing river Avon was not immune from the menace of the world that surrounded it.

This was the world into which Shakespeare was born. England at his birth was still poor and backward, a fringe nation on the periphery of Europe. English itself was a minor language, hardly spoken outside of the country's borders. Religious tension was inescapable, as the old Catholic faith was trying determinedly to hold on, even as Protestantism was once again anxiously trying to establish itself as the national religion. The country knew itself vulnerable to serious threats both from without and from within. In 1562, the young Queen, upon whom so many people's hopes rested, almost fell victim to smallpox, and in 1569 a revolt of the Northern earls tried to remove her from power and restore Catholicism as the national religion. The following year, Pope Pius V pronounced the excommunication of "Elizabeth, the pretended queen of England" and forbade Catholic subjects obedience to the monarch on pain of their own excommunication. "Now we are in an evil way and going to the devil," wrote one clergyman, "and have all nations in our necks."

It was a world of dearth, danger, and domestic unrest. Yet it would soon dramatically change, and Shakespeare's literary contribution would, for future generations, come to be seen as a significant measure of England's remarkable transformation. In the course of Shakespeare's life, England, hitherto an unsophisticated and under-developed backwater acting as a bit player in the momentous political dramas taking place on the European continent, became a confident, prosperous, global presence. But this new world was only accidentally, as it is often known today, "The Age of Shakespeare." To the degree that historical change rests in the hands of any individual, credit must be given to the Queen. This new world arguably was "The Age of Elizabeth," even if it was not the Elizabethan Golden Age, as it has often been portrayed.

The young Queen quickly imposed her personality upon the nation. She had talented councilors around her, all with strong ties to her of friendship or blood, but the direction of government was her own. She was strong willed and cautious, certain of her right to rule and convinced that stability was her greatest responsibility. The result may very well have been, as historians have often charged, that important issues facing England were never dealt with head-on and left to her successors to settle, but it meant also that she was able to keep her England unified and for the most part at peace.

Religion posed her greatest challenge, though it is important to keep in mind that in this period, as an official at Elizabeth's court said, "Religion and the commonwealth cannot be parted asunder." Faith then was not the largely voluntary commitment it is today, nor was there any idea of some separation of church and state. Religion was literally a matter of life and death, of salvation and damnation, and the Church was the Church of England. Obedience to it was not only a matter of conscience but also of law. It was the single issue on which the nation was most likely to be torn apart.

Elizabeth's great achievement was that she was successful in ensuring that the Church of England became formally a Protestant Church, but she did so without either driving most of her Catholic subjects to sedition or alienating the more radical Protestant community. The so-called "Elizabethan Settlement" forged a broad Christian community of what has been called prayer-book Protestantism, even as many of its practitioners retained, as a clergyman said, "still a smack and savor of popish principles." If there were forces on both sides who were uncomfortable with the Settlement—committed Protestants, who wanted to do away with all vestiges of the old faith, and convinced Catholics, who continued to swear their allegiance to Rome—the majority of the country, as she hoped, found ways to live comfortably both within the law and within their faith. In 1571, she wrote to the Duke of Anjou that the forms of worship she recommended would "not properly compel any man to alter his opinion in the great matters now in controversy in the Church." The official toleration of religious ambiguity, as well as the familiar experience of an official change of state religion accompanying the crowning of a new monarch, produced a world where the familiar labels of Protestant and Catholic failed to define the forms of faith that most English people practiced. But for Elizabeth, most matters of faith could be left to individuals, as long as the Church itself, and Elizabeth's position at its head, would remain unchallenged.

In international affairs, she was no less successful with her pragmatism and willingness to pursue limited goals. A complex mix of prudential concerns about religion, the economy, and national security drove her foreign policy. She did not have imperial ambitions; in the main, she wanted only to be sure there would be no invasion of England and to encourage English trade. In the event, both goals brought England into conflict with Spain, determining the increasingly anti-Catholic tendencies of English foreign policy and, almost accidentally, England's emergence as a world power. When Elizabeth came to the throne, England was in many ways a mere satellite nation to the Netherlands, which was part of the Hapsburg Empire that the Catholic Philip II (who had briefly and unhappily been married to her predecessor and half sister, Queen Mary) ruled from Spain; by the end of her reign England was Spain's most bitter rival.

The transformation of Spain from ally to enemy came in a series of small steps (or missteps), no one of which was intended to produce what in the end came to pass. A series of posturings and provocations on both sides led to the rupture. In 1568, things moved to their breaking point, as the English confiscated a large shipment of gold that the Spanish were sending to their troops in the Netherlands. The following year saw the revolt of the Catholic earls in Northern England, followed by the papal excommunication of the Queen in 1570, both of which were by many in England assumed to be at the initiative, or at very least with the tacit support, of Philip. In fact he was not involved, but England under Elizabeth would never again think of Spain as a loyal friend or reliable ally. Indeed, Spain quickly became its mortal enemy. Protestant Dutch rebels had been opposing the Spanish domination of the Netherlands since the early 1560s, but, other than periodic financial support, Elizabeth had done little to encourage them. But in 1585, she sent troops under the command of the Earl of Leicester to support the Dutch rebels against the Spanish. Philip decided then to launch a full-scale attack on England, with the aim of deposing Elizabeth and restoring the Catholic faith. An English assault on Cadiz in 1587 destroyed a number of Spanish ships, postponing Philip's plans, but in the summer of 1588 the mightiest navy in the world, Philip's grand armada, with 132 ships and 30,493 sailors and troops, sailed for England.

By all rights, it should have been a successful invasion, but a combination of questionable Spanish tactics and a fortunate shift of wind resulted in one of England's greatest victories. The English had twice failed to intercept the armada off the coast of Portugal, and the Spanish fleet made its way to England, almost catching the English ships resupplying in Plymouth. The English navy was on its heels, when conveniently the Spanish admiral decided to anchor in the English Channel off the French port of Calais to wait for additional troops coming from the Netherlands. The English attacked with fireships, sinking four Spanish galleons, and strong winds from the south prevented an effective counterattack from the Spanish. The Spanish fleet was pushed into the North Sea, where it regrouped and decided its safest course was to attempt the difficult voyage home around Scotland and Ireland, losing almost half its ships on the way. For many in England the improbable victory was a miracle, evidence of God's favor for Elizabeth and the Protestant nation. Though war with Spain would not end for another fifteen years, the victory over the armada turned England almost overnight into a major world power, buoyed by confidence that they were chosen by God and, more tangibly, by a navy that could compete for control of the seas.

From a backward and insignificant Hapsburg satellite, Elizabeth's England had become, almost by accident, the leader of Protestant Europe. But if the victory over the armada signaled England's new place in the world, it hardly marked the end of England's travails. The economy, which initially was fueled by the military buildup, in the early 1590s fell victim to inflation, heavy taxation to support the war with Spain, the inevitable wartime disruptions of trade, as well as crop failures and a general economic downturn in Europe. Ireland, over which England had been attempting to impose its rule since 1168, continued to be a source of trouble and great expense (in some years costing the crown nearly one fifth of its total revenues). Even when the most organized of the rebellions, begun in 1594 and led by Hugh O'Neill, Earl of Tyrone, formally ended in 1603, peace and stability had not been achieved.

But perhaps the greatest instability came from the uncertainty over the succession, an uncertainty that marked Elizabeth's reign from its beginning. Her near death from smallpox in 1562 reminded the nation that an unmarried queen could not insure the succession, and Elizabeth was under constant pressure to marry and produce an heir. She was always aware of and deeply resented the pressure, announcing as early as 1559: "this shall be for me sufficient that a marble stone shall declare that a queen, having reigned such a time, lived and died a virgin." If, however, it was for her "sufficient," it was not so for her advisors and for much of the nation, who hoped she would wed. Arguably Elizabeth was the wiser, knowing that her unmarried hand was a political advantage, allowing her to diffuse threats or create alliances with the seeming possibility of a match. But as with so much in her reign, the strategy bought temporary stability at the price of longer-term solutions.

By the mid 1590s, it was clear that she would die unmarried and without an heir, and various candidates were positioning themselves to succeed her. Enough anxiety was produced that all published debate about the succession was forbidden by law. There was no direct descendant of the English crown to claim rule, and all the claimants had to reach well back into their family history to find some legitimacy. The best genealogical claim belonged to King James VI of Scotland. His mother, Mary, Queen of Scots, was the granddaughter of James IV of Scotland and Margaret Tudor, sister to Elizabeth's father, Henry VIII. Though James had right on his side, he was, it must be remembered, a foreigner. Scotland shared the island with England but was a separate nation. Great Britain, the union of England and Scotland, would not exist formally until 1707, but with Elizabeth's death early in the morning of March 24, 1603, surprisingly uneventfully the thirty-seven-year-old James succeeded to the English throne. Two nations, one king: King James VI of Scotland, King James I of England.

Most of his English subjects initially greeted the announcement of their new monarch with delight, relieved that the crown had successfully been transferred without any major disruption and reassured that the new King was married with two living sons. However, quickly many became disenchanted with a foreign King who spoke English with a heavy accent, and dismayed even further by the influx of Scots in positions of power. Nonetheless, the new King's greatest political liability may well have been less a matter of nationality than of temperament: he had none of Elizabeth's skill and ease in publicly wooing her subjects. The Venetian ambassador wrote back to the doge that the new King was unwilling to "caress the people, nor make them that good cheer the late Queen did, whereby she won their loves."

He was aloof and largely uninterested in the daily activities of governing, but he was interested in political theory and strongly committed to the cause of peace. Although a steadfast Protestant, he lacked the reflexive anti-Catholicism of many of his subjects. In England, he achieved a broadly consensual community of Protestants. The so-called King James Bible, the famous translation published first in 1611, was the result of a widespread desire to have an English Bible that spoke to all the nation, transcending the religious divisions that had placed three different translations in the hands of his subjects. Internationally, he styled himself *Rex Pacificus* (the peace-loving king). In 1604, the Treaty of London brought Elizabeth's war with Spain formally to an end, and over the next decade he worked to bring about political marriages that might cement stable alliances. In 1613, he married his daughter to the leader of the German Protestants, while the following year he began discussions with Catholic Spain to marry his son to the Infanta Maria. After some ten years of negotiations, James's hopes for what was known as the Spanish match were finally abandoned, much to the delight of the nation, whose long-felt fear and hatred for Spain outweighed the subtle political logic behind the plan.

But if James sought stability and peace, and for the most part succeeded in his aims (at least until 1618, when the bitter religio-political conflicts on the European continent swirled well out of the

King's control), he never really achieved concord and cohesion. He ruled over two kingdoms that did not know, like, or even want to understand one another, and his rule did little to bring them closer together. His England remained separate from his Scotland, even as he ruled over both. And even his England remained self divided, as in truth it always was under Elizabeth, ever more a nation of prosperity and influence but still one forged out of deep-rooted divisions of means, faiths, and allegiances that made the very nature of English identity a matter of confusion and concern. Arguably this is the very condition of great drama—sufficient peace and prosperity to support a theater industry and sufficient provocation in the troubling uncertainties about what the nation was and what fundamentally mattered to its people to inspire plays that would offer tentative solutions or at the very least make the troubling questions articulate and moving.

Nine years before James would die in 1625, Shakespeare died, having returned from London to the small market town in which he was born. If London, now a thriving modern metropolis of well over 200,000 people, had, like the nation itself, been transformed in the course of his life, the Warwickshire market town still was much the same. The house in which Shakespeare was born still stood, as did the church in which he was baptized and the school in which he learned to read and write. The river Avon still ran slowly along the town's southern limits. What had changed was that Shakespeare was now its most famous citizen, and, although it would take more than another 100 years to fully achieve this, he would in time become England's, for having turned the great ethical, social, and political issues of his own age into plays that would live forever.

William Shakespeare: A Chronology

1558	**November 17: Queen Elizabeth crowned**
1564	April 26: Shakespeare baptized, third child born to John Shakespeare and Mary Arden
1564	**May 27: Death of Jean Calvin in Geneva**
1565	John Shakespeare elected alderman in Stratford-upon-Avon
1568	**Publication of the Bishops' Bible**
1568	September 4: John Shakespeare elected Bailiff of Stratford-upon-Avon
1569	**Northern Rebellion**
1570	**Queen Elizabeth excommunicated by the Pope**
1572	**August 24: St. Bartholomew's Day Massacre in Paris**
1576	**The Theatre is built in Shoreditch**
1577–1580	**Sir Francis Drake sails around the world**
1582	November 27: Shakespeare and Anne Hathaway married (Shakespeare is 18)
1583	Queen's Men formed
1583	May 26: Shakespeare's daughter, Susanna, baptized
1584	**Failure of the Virginia Colony**

1585   February 2: Twins, Hamnet and Judith, baptized (Shakespeare is 20)

1586   Babington Plot to dethrone Elizabeth and replace her with Mary, Queen of Scots

1587   February 8: Execution of Mary, Queen of Scots

1587   Rose Theatre built

1588   August: Defeat of the Spanish armada (Shakespeare is 24)

1588   September 4: Death of Robert Dudley, Earl of Leicester

1590   First three books of Spenser's *Faerie Queene* published; Marlowe's *Tamburlaine* published

1592   March 3: *Henry VI, Part One* performed at the Rose Theatre (Shakespeare is 27)

1593   February–November: Theaters closed because of plague

1593   Publication of *Venus and Adonis*

1594   Publication of *Titus Andronicus*, first play by Shakespeare to appear in print (though anonymously)

1594   Lord Chamberlain's Men formed

1595   March 15: Payment made to Shakespeare, Will Kemp, and Richard Burbage for performances at court in December, 1594

1595   Swan Theatre built

1596   Books 4–6 of *The Faerie Queene* published

1596   August 11: Burial of Shakespeare's son, Hamnet (Shakespeare is 32)

1596–1599   Shakespeare living in St. Helen's, Bishopsgate, London

1596   October 20: Grant of Arms to John Shakespeare

1597   May 4: Shakespeare purchases New Place, one of the two largest houses in Stratford (Shakespeare is 33)

1598   Publication of *Love's Labor's Lost*, first extant play with Shakespeare's name on the title page

1598   Publication of Francis Meres's *Palladis Tamia*, citing Shakespeare as "the best for Comedy and Tragedy" among English writers

1599   Opening of the Globe Theatre

1601   February 7: Lord Chamberlain's Men paid 40 shillings to play *Richard II* by supporters of the Earl of Essex, the day before his abortive rebellion

1601   February 17: Execution of Robert Devereaux, Earl of Essex

1601   September 8: Burial of John Shakespeare

1602   May 1: Shakespeare buys 107 acres of farmland in Stratford

1603   March 24: Queen Elizabeth dies; James VI of Scotland succeeds as James I of England (Shakespeare is 39)

1603   May 19: Lord Chamberlain's Men reformed as the King's Men

1604   Shakespeare living with the Mountjoys, a French Huguenot family, in Cripplegate, London

1604   First edition of Marlowe's *Dr. Faustus* published (written c. 1589)

1604   March 15: Shakespeare named among "players" given scarlet cloth to wear at royal procession of King James

1604   Publication of authorized version of *Hamlet* (Shakespeare is 40)

1605   Gunpowder Plot

1605   June 5: Marriage of Susanna Shakespeare to John Hall

1608   Publication of *King Lear* (Shakespeare is 44)

1608–1609   Acquisition of indoor Blackfriars Theatre by King's Men

1609	*Sonnets* published
1611	**King James Bible published** (Shakespeare is 47)
1612	**November 6: Death of Henry, eldest son of King James**
1613	**February 14: Marriage of King James's daughter Elizabeth to Frederick, the Elector Palatine**
1613	March 10: Shakespeare, with some associates, buys gatehouse in Blackfriars, London
1613	**June 29: Fire burns the Globe Theatre**
1614	**Rebuilt Globe reopens**
1616	February 10: Marriage of Judith Shakespeare to Thomas Quiney
1616	March 25: Shakespeare's will signed
1616	April 23: Shakespeare dies (age 52)
1616	**April 23: Cervantes dies in Madrid**
1616	April 25: Shakespeare buried in Holy Trinity Church in Stratford-upon-Avon
1623	August 6: Death of Anne Shakespeare
1623	**October: Prince Charles, King James's son, returns from Madrid, having failed to arrange his marriage to Maria Anna, Infanta of Spain**
1623	First Folio published with 36 plays (18 never previously published)

Words, Words, Words: Understanding Shakespeare's Language

by David Scott Kastan

t is silly to pretend that it is easy to read Shakespeare. Reading Shakespeare isn't like picking up a copy of *USA Today* or *The New Yorker*, or even F. Scott Fitzgerald's *Great Gatsby* or Toni Morrison's *Beloved*. It is hard work, because the language is often unfamiliar to us and because it is more concentrated than we are used to. In the theater it is usually a bit easier. Actors can clarify meanings with gestures and actions, allowing us to get the general sense of what is going on, if not every nuance of the language that is spoken. "Action is eloquence," as Volumnia puts it in *Coriolanus*, "and the eyes of th' ignorant / More learnèd than the ears" (3.276–277). Yet the real greatness of Shakespeare rests not on "the general sense" of his plays but on the specificity and suggestiveness of the words in which they are written. It is through language that the plays' full dramatic power is realized, and it is that rich and robust language, often pushed by Shakespeare to the very limits of intelligibility, that we must learn to understand. But we can come to understand it (and enjoy it), and this essay is designed to help.

Even experienced readers and playgoers need help. They often find that his words are difficult to comprehend. Shakespeare sometimes uses words no longer current in English or with meanings that have changed. He regularly multiplies words where seemingly one might do as well or even better. He characteristically writes sentences that are syntactically complicated and imaginatively dense. And it isn't just we, removed by some 400 years from his world, who find him difficult to read; in his own time, his friends and fellow actors knew Shakespeare was hard. As two of them, John Hemings and Henry Condell, put it in their prefatory remarks to Shakespeare's First Folio in 1623, "read him, therefore, and again and again; and if then you do not like him, surely you are in some manifest danger not to understand him."

From the very beginning, then, it was obvious that the plays both deserve and demand not only careful reading but continued re-reading—and that not to read Shakespeare with all the attention a reader can bring to bear on the language is almost to guarantee that a reader will not "understand him" and remain among those who "do not like him." But Shakespeare's colleagues were nonetheless confident that the plays exerted an attraction strong enough to ensure and reward the concentration of their readers, confident, as they say, that in them "you will find enough, both to draw and hold you." The plays do exert a kind of magnetic pull, and have successfully drawn in and held readers for over 400 years.

Once we are drawn in, we confront a world of words that does not always immediately yield its delights; but it will—once we learn to see what is demanded of us. Words in Shakespeare do a lot, arguably more than anyone else has ever asked them to do. In part, it is because he needed his words to do many things at once. His stage had no sets and few props, so his words are all we have to enable us to imagine what his characters see. And they also allow us to see what the characters don't see, especially about themselves. The words are vivid and immediate, as well as complexly layered and psychologically suggestive. The difficulties they pose are not the "thee's" and "thou's" or "prithee's" and "doth's" that obviously mark the chronological distance between Shakespeare and us. When

Gertrude says to Hamlet, "thou hast thy father much offended" (3.4.8), we have no difficulty understanding her chiding, though we might miss that her use of the "thou" form of the pronoun expresses an intimacy that Hamlet pointedly refuses with his reply: "Mother, *you* have my father much offended" (3.4.9; italics mine).

Most deceptive are words that look the same as words we know but now mean something different. Words often change meanings over time. When Horatio and the soldiers try to stop Hamlet as he chases after the Ghost, Hamlet pushes past them and says, "I'll make a ghost of him that lets me" (1.4.85). It seems an odd thing to say. Why should he threaten someone who "lets" him do what he wants to do? But here "let" means "hinder," not, as it does today, "allow" (although the older meaning of the word still survives, for example, in tennis, where a "let serve" is one that is hindered by the net on its way across). There are many words that can, like this, mislead us: "his" sometimes means "its," "an" often means "if," "envy" means something more like "malice," "cousin" means more generally "kinsman," and there are others, though all are easily defined. The difficulty is that we may not stop to look thinking we already know what the word means, but in this edition a ° following the word alerts a reader that there is a gloss in the left margin, and quickly readers get used to these older meanings.

Then, of course, there is the intimidation factor—strange, polysyllabic, or Latinate words that not only are foreign to us but also must have sounded strange even to Shakespeare's audiences. When Macbeth wonders whether all the water in all the oceans of the world will be able to clean his bloody hands after the murder of Duncan, he concludes: "No; this my hand will rather / The multitudinous seas incarnadine, / Making the green one red" (2.2.64–66). Duncan's blood staining Macbeth's murderous hand is so offensive that, not merely does it resist being washed off in water, but it will "the multitudinous seas incarnadine": that is, turn the sea-green oceans blood-red. Notes will easily clarify the meaning of the two odd words, but it is worth observing that they would have been as odd to Shakespeare's readers as they are to us. The *Oxford English Dictionary* (*OED*) shows no use of "multitudinous" before this, and it records no use of "incarnadine" before 1591 (*Macbeth* was written about 1606). Both are new words, coined from the Latin, part of a process in Shakespeare's time where English adopted many Latinate words as a mark of its own emergence as an important vernacular language. Here they are used to express the magnitude of Macbeth's offense, a crime not only against the civil law but also against the cosmic order, and then the simple monosyllables of turning "the green one red" provide an immediate (and needed) paraphrase and register his own sickening awareness of the true hideousness of his deed.

As with "multitudinous" in *Macbeth*, Shakespeare is the source of a great many words in English. Sometimes he coined them himself, or, if he didn't invent them, he was the first person whose writing of them has survived. Some of these words have become part of our language, so common that it is hard to imagine they were not always part of it: for example, "assassination" (*Macbeth*, 1.7.2), "bedroom" (*A Midsummer Night's Dream*, 2.2.57), "countless" (*Titus Andronicus*, 5.3.59), "fashionable" (*Troilus and Cressida*, 3.3.165), "frugal" (*The Merry Wives of Windsor*, 2.1.28), "laughable" (*The Merchant of Venice*, 1.1.56), "lonely" (*Coriolanus*, 4.1.30), and "useful" (*King John*, 5.2.81). But other words that he originated were not as, to use yet another Shakespearean coinage, "successful" (*Titus Andronicus*, 1.1.66). Words like "crimeless" (*Henry VI, Part Two*, 2.4.63, meaning "innocent"), "facinorous" (*All's Well That Ends Well*, 2.3.30, meaning "extremely wicked"), and "recountment" (*As You Like It*, 4.3.141, meaning "narrative" or "account") have, without much resistance, slipped into oblivion. Clearly Shakespeare liked words, even unwieldy ones. His working vocabulary, about 18,000 words, is staggering, larger than almost any other English writer, and he seems to be the first person to use in print about

1,000 of these. Whether he coined the new words himself or was intrigued by the new words he heard in the streets of London doesn't really matter; the point is that he was remarkably alert to and engaged with a dynamic language that was expanding in response to England's own expanding contact with the world around it.

But it is neither new words nor old ones that are the source of the greatest difficulty of Shakespeare's language. The real difficulty (and the real delight) comes in trying to see how he uses the words, how he endows them with more than their denotative meanings. Why, for example, does Macbeth say that he hopes that the "sure and firm-set earth" (2.1.56) will not hear his steps as he goes forward to murder Duncan? Here "sure" and "firm-set" mean virtually the same thing: stable, secure, fixed. Why use two words? If this were a student paper, no doubt the teacher would circle one of them and write "redundant." But the redundancy is exactly what Shakespeare wants. One word would do if the purpose were to describe the solidity of the earth, but here the redundancy points to something different. It reveals something about Macbeth's mind, betraying through the doubling how deep is his awareness of the world of stable values that the terrible act he is about to commit must unsettle.

Shakespeare's words usually work this way: in part describing what the characters see and as often betraying what they feel. The example from *Macbeth* is a simple example of how this works. Shakespeare's words are carefully patterned. How one says something is every bit as important as what is said, and the conspicuous patterns that are created alert us to the fact that something more than the words' lexical sense has been put into play. Words can be coupled, as in the example above, or knit into even denser metaphorical constellations to reveal something about the speaker (which often the speaker does not know), as in Prince Hal's promise to his father that he will outdo the rebels' hero, Henry Percy (Hotspur):

Percy is but my factor, good my lord,

To engross up glorious deeds on my behalf.

And I will call him to so strict account

That he shall render every glory up,

Yea, even the slightest worship of his time,

Or I will tear the reckoning from his heart.

(Henry IV, Part One, 3.2.147–152)

The Prince expresses his confidence that he will defeat Hotspur, but revealingly in a reiterated language of commercial exchange ("factor," "engross," "account," "render," "reckoning") that tells us something important both about the Prince and the ways in which he understands his world. In a play filled with references to coins and counterfeiting, the speech demonstrates not only that Hal has committed himself to the business at hand, repudiating his earlier, irresponsible tavern self, but also that he knows it is a business rather than a glorious world of chivalric achievement; he inhabits a world in which value (political as well as economic) is not intrinsic but determined by what people are willing to invest, and he proves himself a master of producing desire for what he has to offer.

Or sometimes it is not the network of imagery but the very syntax that speaks, as when Claudius announces his marriage to Hamlet's mother:

Therefore our sometime sister, now our Queen,

Th' imperial jointress to this warlike state,

Have we—as 'twere with a defeated joy,

With an auspicious and a dropping eye,

With mirth in funeral and with dole in marriage,

In equal scale weighing delight and dole—

Taken to wife.   *(Hamlet, 1.2.8–14)*

All he really wants to say here is that he has married Gertrude, his former sister-in-law: "Therefore our sometime sister . . . Have we . . . Taken to wife." But the straightforward sentence gets interrupted and complicated, revealing his own discomfort with the announcement. His elaborations and intensifications of Gertrude's role ("sometime sister," "Queen," "imperial jointress"), the self-conscious rhetorical balancing of the middle three lines (indeed "in equal scale weighing delight and dole"), all declare by the all-too obvious artifice how desperate he is to hide the awkward facts behind a veneer of normalcy and propriety. The very unnaturalness of the sentence is what alerts us that we are meant to understand more than the simple relation of fact.

Why doesn't Shakespeare just say what he means? Well, he does—exactly what he means. In the example from *Hamlet* just above, Shakespeare shows us something about Claudius that Claudius doesn't know himself. Always Shakespeare's words will offer us an immediate sense of what is happening, allowing us to follow the action, but they also offer us a counterplot, pointing us to what might be behind the action, confirming or contradicting what the characters say. It is a language that shimmers with promise and possibility, opening the characters' hearts and minds to our view—and all we have to do is learn to pay attention to what is there before us.

Shakespeare's Verse

Another distinctive feature of Shakespeare's dramatic language is that much of it is in verse. Almost all of the plays mix poetry and prose, but the poetry dominates. *The Merry Wives of Windsor* has the lowest percentage (only about 13 percent verse), while *Richard II* and *King John* are written entirely in verse (the only examples, although *Henry VI, Part One* and *Part Three* have only a very few prose lines). In most of the plays, about 70 percent of the lines are written in verse.

Shakespeare's characteristic verse line is a non-rhyming iambic pentameter ("blank verse"), ten syllables with every second one stressed. In *A Midsummer Night's Dream*, Titania comes to her senses after a magic potion has led her to fall in love with an ass-headed Bottom: "Methought I was enamored of an ass" (4.1.76). Similarly, in *Romeo and Juliet*, Romeo gazes up at Juliet's window: "But soft, what light through yonder window breaks" (2.2.2). In both these examples, the line has ten syllables organized into five regular beats (each beat consisting of the stress on the second syllable of a pair, as in "But soft," the da-dum rhythm forming an "iamb"). Still, we don't hear these lines as jingles; they seem natural enough, in large part because this dominant pattern is varied in the surrounding lines.

The play of stresses indeed becomes another key to meaning, as Shakespeare alerts us to what is important. In *Measure for Measure*, Lucio urges Isabella to plead for her brother's life: "Oh, to him, to him, wench! He will relent" (2.2.129). The iambic norm (unstressed-stressed) tells us (and an actor) that the emphasis at the beginning of the line is on "to" not "him"—it is the action not the object that is being emphasized—and at the end of the line the stress falls on "will." Alternatively, the line can play against the established norm. In *Hamlet*, Claudius corrects Polonius's idea of what is bothering the Prince: "Love? His affections do not that way tend" (3.1.161). The iambic norm forces the emphasis onto "that" ("do not *that* way tend"), while the syntax forces an unexpected stress on the opening word, "Love." In the famous line, "The course of true love never did run smooth" (*A Midsummer Night's Dream*, 1.1.134), the iambic expectation is varied in both the middle and at the end of the line. Both "love" and the first syllable of "never" are stressed, as are both syllables at the end: "run smooth," creating a metrical foot in which both syllables are stressed (called a "spondee"). The point to notice is that the "da-dum, da-dum, da-dum, da-dum, da-dum" line is not inevitable; it merely sets an expectation against which many variations can be heard.

In fact, even the ten-syllable norm can be varied. Shakespeare sometimes writes lines with fewer or more syllables. Often there is an extra, unstressed syllable at the end of a line (a so-called "feminine ending"); sometimes there are verse lines with only nine. In *Henry IV, Part One*, King Henry replies incredulously to the rebel Worcester's claim that he hadn't "sought" the confrontation with the King: "You have not sought it. How comes it then?" (5.1.27). There are only nine syllables here (some earlier editors, seeking to "correct" the verse, added the word "sir" after the first question to regularize the line). But the pause where one expects a stressed syllable is dramatically effective, allowing the King's anger to be powerfully present in the silence.

As even these few examples show, Shakespeare's verse is unusually flexible, allowing a range of rhythmical effects. It should not be understood as a set of strict rules but as a flexible set of practices rooted in dramatic necessity. It is designed to highlight ideas and emotions, and it is based less upon rigid syllable counts than on an arrangement of stresses within an understood temporal norm, as one might expect from a poetry written to be heard in the theater rather than read on the page.

Here Follows Prose

Although the plays are dominated by verse, prose plays a significant role. Shakespeare's prose has its own rhythms, but it lacks the formal patterning of verse, and so is printed without line breaks and without the capitals that mark the beginning of a verse line. Like many of his fellow dramatists, Shakespeare tended to use prose for comic scenes, the shift from verse serving, especially in his early plays, as a social marker. Upper-class characters speak in verse; lower-class characters speak in prose. Thus, in *A Midsummer Night's Dream*, the Athenians of the court, as well as the fairies, all speak in verse, but the "rude mechanicals," Bottom and his artisan friends, all speak in prose, except for the comic verse they speak in their performance of "Pyramis and Thisbe."

As Shakespeare grew in experience, he became more flexible about the shifts from verse to prose, letting it, among other things, mark genre rather than class and measure various kinds of intensity. Prose becomes in the main the medium of comedy. The great comedies, like *Much Ado About Nothing*, *Twelfth Night*, and *As You Like It*, are all more than 50 percent prose. But even in comedy, shifts between verse and prose may be used to measure subtle emotional changes. In Act One, scene three of *The Merchant of Venice*, Shylock and Bassanio begin the scene speaking of matters of business in prose, but when Antonio enters and the deep conflict between the Christian and the Jew becomes evident, the scene shifts to verse. But prose may itself serve in moments of emotional intensity. Shylock's famous speech in Act Three, scene one, "Hath not a Jew eyes . . ." is all in prose, as is Hamlet's expression of disgust at the world ("I have of late—but wherefore I know not—lost all my mirth . . .") at 3.1.261–276. Shakespeare comes to use prose to vary the tone of a scene, as the shift from verse subtly alerts an audience or a reader to some new emotional register.

Prose becomes, as Shakespeare's art matures, not inevitably the mark of the lower classes but the mark of a salutary daily-ness. It is appropriately the medium in which letters are written, and it is the medium of a common sense that will at least challenge the potential self-deceptions of grandiloquent speech. When Rosalind mocks the excesses and artifice of Orlando's wooing in Act Four, scene one of *As You Like It*, it is in prose that she seeks something genuine in the expression of love:

The poor world is almost six thousand years old, and in all this time there was not any man died in his own person, *videlicit* [i.e., namely], in a love cause. . . . Men have died from time to time, and worms have eaten them, but not for love.

Here the prose becomes the sound of common sense, an effective foil to the affectation of pinning poems to trees and thinking that it is real love.

It is not that prose is artless; Shakespeare's prose is no less self-conscious than his verse. The artfulness of his prose is different, of course. The seeming ordinariness of his prose is no less an effect of his artistry than is the more obvious patterning of his verse. Prose is no less serious, compressed, or indeed figurative. As with his verse, Shakespeare's prose performs numerous tasks and displays various, subtle formal qualities; and recognizing the possibilities of what it can achieve is still another way of seeing what Shakespeare puts right before us to show us what he has hidden.

Further Reading

N.F. Blake, *Shakespeare's Language: An Introduction* (New York: St. Martin's Press, 1983).

Jonathan Hope, *Shakespeare's Grammar* (London: Thomson, 2003).

Sister Miriam Joseph, *Shakespeare's Use of the Arts of Language* (New York: Columbia University Press, 1947).

M. M. Mahood, *Shakespeare's Wordplay* (London: Methuen, 1957).

Russ McDonald, *Shakespeare and the Arts of Language* (Oxford: Oxford University Press, 2001).

Brian Vickers, *The Artistry of Shakespeare's Prose* (London: Methuen, 1968).

George T. Wright, *Shakespeare's Metrical Art* (Berkeley: Univ. of California Press, 1991).

Key to the Play Text

Symbols

o   Indicates an explanation or definition in the left-hand margin.

1   Indicates a gloss on the page facing the play text.

[ ]   Indicates something added or changed by the editors (i.e., not in the early printed text that this edition of the play is based on).

Terms

F, Folio, or *First Folio*	The first collected edition of Shakespeare's plays, published in 1623. *Twelfth Night* was first published in the First Folio.
Q, Quarto	The usual format in which the individual plays were first published.

Twelfth Night

subtitle "What you will"

William Shakespeare

List of Roles

Viola	*a shipwrecked Lady of Messaline (later disguised as Cesario)*
Orsino	*Duke of Illyria*
Valentine	*a gentleman of Orsino's household*
Curio	*a gentleman of Orsino's household*
Olivia	*a Countess of Illyria*
Maria	*a gentlewoman of Olivia's household*
Sir Toby Belch	*Olivia's uncle*
Sir Andrew Aguecheek	*a friend of Sir Toby's*
Malvolio	*Olivia's steward*
Feste	*a clown, Olivia's jester*
Fabian	*a gentleman of Olivia's household*
Servant	
Sebastian	*Viola's twin brother*
Antonio	*a sea captain and friend of Sebastian*
Sea Captain	*rescuer of Viola*
Priest	
First Officer	
Second Officer	

Lords, sailors, officers, attendants, and musicians

1 *a dying fall*

An ending cadence (*fall*) with a rhythm, or perhaps a harmony, that is sad or poignant.

2 *like the sweet sound / That breathes upon a bank of violets, / Stealing and giving odor*

Like a breeze that blows across a field of violets, taking the scent from some flowers and carrying it to others

3 *validity and pitch*

Value and excellence (*pitch* is the apex of a falcon's flight)

4 *notwithstanding thy capacity / Receiveth as the sea, naught enters there, / Of what validity and pitch soe'er, / But falls into abatement and low price / Even in a minute*

Even though you can absorb as much as the sea, everything that comes your way—no matter how valuable—quickly becomes worthless.

5 *So full of shapes is fancy / That it alone is high fantastical.*

Love can manifest itself in so many different forms that it is the only true imaginative power.

6 *hart*

Stag; in his next line, Orsino puns on *hart* and *heart*.

7 *purged the air of pestilence*

Cleared the air of plague (believed to be transmitted through the air)

8 *That instant was I turned into a hart, / And my desires, like fell and cruel hounds, / E'er since pursue me.*

An allusion to Actaeon, a hunter from Greek mythology, depicted in Book 3 of Ovid's *Metamorphoses*. As a punishment for having seen the goddess Diana naked, Actaeon was transformed into a stag before being hunted down by his own dogs. Diana was the goddess of chastity, renowned for her contempt for love and passion for hunting. In Renaissance literature, Actaeon was usually an emblem for the comic figure of the *cuckold*, a man thought to grow horns on his head because his wife was unfaithful to him. Orsino emphasizes the pathos in Actaeon's plight, that of a man undone by his own creatures' failure to recognize him. There were a number of Renaissance songs about Diana, one of which, if played here, could provide an additional context for these remarks. See APPENDIX: The Songs of *Twelfth Night*, page 285.

Act 1, Scene 1

Enter **Orsino**, *Duke of Illyria*, **Curio**, *and other lords.*
[Musicians play.]

Orsino

[*smitten w/ olivia*]   [*Violia & Sebestain brother+sister*]

If music be the food of love, play on.

having too much   Give me excess of it that, surfeiting,°

The appetite may sicken and so die.

musical passage   That strain° again—it had a dying fall. [1]

Oh, it came o'er my ear like the sweet sound   5

That breathes upon a bank of violets,

Stealing and giving odor. [2] Enough, no more.

'Tis not so sweet now as it was before. [*Music stops.*]

eager   O spirit of love, how quick and fresh° art thou,

That, notwithstanding thy capacity   10

Receiveth as the sea, naught enters there,

Of what validity and pitch [3] soe'er,

But falls into abatement and low price

love   Even in a minute. [4] So full of shapes is fancy°

That it alone is high fantastical. [5]   15

Curio

Will you go hunt, my lord?

Orsino

                What, Curio?

Curio

                          The hart. [6]

Orsino

Why, so I do, the noblest that I have.

Oh, when mine eyes did see Olivia first,

Methought she purged the air of pestilence. [7]

That instant was I turned into a hart,   20

ferocious   And my desires, like fell° and cruel hounds,

E'er since pursue me. [8]

1   *The element itself, till seven years' heat*
    **I.e., the sky itself, for seven
    summers**

2   *to season / A brother's dead love*
    **To keep fresh the memory of a
    beloved dead brother. Olivia's
    tears will keep her brother's
    memory alive, just as salty brine
    preserves meat or vegetables.**

3   *when the rich golden shaft / Hath killed the
    flock of all affections else / That live in her*
    **When Cupid's golden-shafted
    arrow (which causes its targets to
    fall passionately in love) kills all
    her other emotions**

4   *liver, brain, and heart*
    **In the Renaissance, the liver, along
    with the brain and heart, was
    considered one of the three seats
    of love; it played a key role in
    producing telltale signs of love-
    sickness, such as pallor, weight
    loss, hollow eyes, and insomnia.
    Though Orsino here imagines the
    happy prospect of Olivia's organs
    responding to him, later, when
    discussing the relative feebleness
    of a woman's capacity for love, he
    dismisses female loving as *No
    motion of the liver, but the palate, / That
    suffer surfeit, cloyment, and revolt*
    (2.4.97–98).**

5   *filled / Her sweet perfections with one self
    king*
    **I.e., her sweet perfections filled
    with but a single master (Orsino)**

6   *bowers*
    **Frameworks that support plants;
    arbors**

Enter **Valentine**.

                                        How now! What news from her?
Valentine

let in   So please my lord, I might not be admitted,°
                But from her handmaid do return this answer:
                The element itself, till seven years' heat, [1]   25
full   Shall not behold her face at ample° view,   olivia just lost
nun   But like a cloistress° she will veilèd walk   brother, mourning,
                And water once a day her chamber round   will wear all
tears   With eye-offending brine°—all this to season   black
                A brother's dead love, [2] which she would keep fresh   30
                And lasting in her sad remembrance.
Orsino

excellently built   Oh, she that hath a heart of that fine° frame
only   To pay this debt of love but° to a brother,
                How will she love when the rich golden shaft
                Hath killed the flock of all affections else   35
                That live in her [3] —when liver, brain, and heart, [4]
                These sovereign thrones, are all supplied, and filled
                Her sweet perfections with one self king! [5]
                Away before me to sweet beds of flowers.
                Love thoughts lie rich when canopied with bowers. [6]   40
                                                            They exit.

1   *Elysium*

    Heaven, in Greek mythology

2   *chance*

    What might have taken place

3   *our driving boat*

    The ship's lifeboat, driven along by
    the storm

4   *Most provident in peril*

    Extremely prudent and foresighted,
    despite being in danger

5   *like Arion on the dolphin's back*

    Refers to a Greek legend of a
    musician who jumped off a ship
    when he learned he was to be
    murdered; a dolphin, charmed by
    his singing voice, brought him
    safely to shore.

6   *hold acquaintance with the waves*

    I.e., continue to stay afloat

7   *Mine own escape unfoldeth to my hope, /
    Whereto thy speech serves for authority, /
    The like of him.*

    The fact that I escaped gives me
    hope—which your account
    encourages—that my brother has
    survived as well.

Act 1, Scene 2

Enter **Viola**, *a* **Captain**, *and sailors.*

Viola

What country, friends, is this?

Captain

                    This is Illyria, lady.

Viola

And what should I do in Illyria?

My brother he is in Elysium. [1]

Perhaps   Perchance° he is not drowned.—What think you, sailors?

Captain

only by chance   It is perchance° that you yourself were saved.   5

Viola

Oh, my poor brother! And so perchance may he be.

Captain *saw viola's brother in trouble at sea*

True, madam; and, to comfort you with chance, [2]

Assure yourself, after our ship did split,

When you and those poor number saved with you

Hung on our driving boat, [3] I saw your brother,   10

Most provident in peril, [4] bind himself—

Courage and hope both teaching him the practice—

floated   To a strong mast that lived° upon the sea,

Where, like Arion on the dolphin's back, [5]

I saw him hold acquaintance with the waves [6]   15

So long as I could see.

Viola

            [*giving him coins*] For saying so, there's gold.

Mine own escape unfoldeth to my hope,

Whereto thy speech serves for authority,

The like of him. [7] Know'st thou this country?

1   *fresh in murmur*

   The topic of new gossip

Captain

Ay, madam, well, for I was bred and born   20
Not three hours' travel from this very place.

Viola

Who governs here?

Captain

               A noble Duke, in nature
As in name.

Viola

          What is his name?

Captain

                  Orsino.

Viola

Orsino. I have heard my father name him.
He was a bachelor then.   25

Captain

recently And so is now, or was so very late,°
For but a month ago I went from hence,
And then 'twas fresh in murmur[1]—as, you know,
lower classes What great ones do the less° will prattle of—
That he did seek the love of fair Olivia.   30

Viola

What's she?

↳ dad & brother died

Captain

A virtuous maid, the daughter of a count
That died some twelvemonth since, then leaving her
In the protection of his son, her brother,
Who shortly also died, for whose dear love,   35
sworn off They say, she hath abjured° the sight
And company of men.

Viola

                Oh, that I served that lady
revealed And might not be delivered° to the world,

1	*And might not be delivered to the world, /
	Till I had made mine own occasion
	mellow, / What my estate is*

	**And could avoid revealing to the
	world my condition until I had
	made myself ready**

2	*though that*

	Although

3	*close in*

	Conceal

4	*as haply shall become / The form of my
	intent*

	That with luck will suit my plans

5	*Thou shalt present me as an eunuch to him.*

	**Viola here imagines her disguise as
	that of a eunuch or *castrato*, a male
	soprano who might appeal to the
	music-loving Orsino or as one of
	the eunuchs that served as guards
	in Turkish harems. The Captain in
	line 58 takes it in this latter sense
	(See LONGER NOTE on page 287).**

6	*to time I will commit*

	I'll give over to fate.

7	*mute*

	**Mutes, low-ranking servants at one
	time employed in Turkish courts,
	had their tongues cut out to ensure
	their silence about what they saw.**

ripe Till I had made mine own occasion mellow,°
What my estate is. [1]
Captain
achieve   That were hard to compass,°   40
solicitation Because she will admit no kind of suit,°
No, not the Duke's.
Viola
There is a fair behavior in thee, captain,
And though that[2] nature with a beauteous wall
Doth oft close in[3] pollution, yet of thee   45
I will believe thou hast a mind that suits
appearance With this thy fair and outward character.°
I prithee—and I'll pay thee bounteously—
Conceal me what I am and be my aid
For such disguise as haply shalt become   50
The form of my intent.[4] I'll serve this Duke.
Thou shall present me as an eunuch to him.[5]
It may be worth thy pains, for I can sing   *will be disguised as a man*
And speak to him in many sorts of music
prove That will allow° me very worth his service.   55
happen What else may hap,° to time I will commit.[6]
imagination Only shape thou thy silence to my wit.°
Captain
Be you his eunuch, and your mute[7] I'll be.
When my tongue blabs, then let mine eyes not see.
Viola
I thank thee. Lead me on.   *They exit.* 60

1   *What a plague*

I.e., what the devil; a common
imprecation

2   *cousin*

An unspecific term for a relative;
Olivia is actually Sir Toby's niece.

3   *let her except before excepted*

A pun on the legal term *exceptis
excipiendis*, meaning "with the
already noted exceptions." Toby's
general sense is, "I don't care if she
takes exception."

4   *I'll confine myself no finer than I am.*

(1) I'll not dress in clothes above my
social station; (2) I'll not confine
myself to a narrower body than I have
(i.e., I refuse to lose any weight).

5   *tall*

Valiant, worthy. Maria takes the
word in its more usual sense, as a
reference to Sir Andrew's stature.

6   *What's that to th' purpose?*

I.e., what's that got to do with
anything? Maria is the butt of jokes
about her small size, hence her
sensitivity here.

Act 1, Scene 3

Enter **Sir Toby [Belch]** *and* **Maria**.

Sir Toby Belch

_{→ olivia's cousin, drunk most of the time}

What a plague [1] means my niece to take the death of
worry is her brother thus? I am sure care's° an enemy to life.

Maria

faith By my troth,° Sir Toby, you must come in earlier o'
nights. Your cousin, [2] my lady, takes great exceptions to
your ill hours.   5

Sir Toby Belch

Why, let her except before excepted. [3]

Maria

moderate Ay, but you must confine yourself within the modest°
limits of order.

Sir Toby Belch

Confine? I'll confine myself no finer than I am. [4] These
clothes are good enough to drink in, and so be these   10
If boots too. An° they be not, let them hang themselves
in their own straps.

Maria

guzzling That quaffing° and drinking will undo you. I heard my
lady talk of it yesterday, and of a foolish knight that you
brought in one night here to be her wooer.   15

Sir Toby Belch

Who? Sir Andrew Aguecheek?

Maria

Ay, he.

Sir Toby Belch

He's as tall [5] a man as any 's in Illyria.

Maria

What's that to th' purpose? [6]

1   *but he'll have but a year in all these ducats*
    But he'll spend all those ducats in a year.

2   *viol-de-gamboys*
    An odd, perhaps drunken pronunciation of *viola da gamba*, a stringed instrument similar to a cello, held between the legs when played

3   *without book*
    From memory

4   *almost natural*
    ***Natural* could be used as a synonym for "imbecile" or "idiot."**

5   *but that he hath the gift of a coward to allay the gust he hath in quarreling*
    If it weren't for the fact that he has a talent for cowardice to compensate for the gusto he has for starting fights

6   *substractors*
    A mispronunciation of *detractors*. In her next line, Maria makes a pun based on "subtract," her correction of *substract*.

7   *coistrel*
    Knave (literally a horse groom)

8   *turn o' th' toe like a parish top*
    Spin around like a large top. "Parish tops" were spun by whipping and often kept by parishes for exercise and recreation.

9   Castiliano vulgo
    Possibly a phase similar to "Speak of the Devil!" The precise meaning of this apparently Spanish expression is unknown.

Sir Toby Belch

Why, he has three thousand ducats a year.   20

Maria

Ay, but he'll have but a year in all these ducats.[1] He's a
utter / spendthrift   very° fool and a prodigal.°

Sir Toby Belch

Fie that you'll say so! He plays o' the viol-de-gamboys,[2]
and speaks three or four languages word for word without book,[3] and hath all the good gifts of nature.   25

Maria

He hath indeed, almost natural,[4] for besides that he's a
fool, he's a great quarreler, and, but that he hath the
gift of a coward to allay the gust he hath in quarreling,[5]
'tis thought among the prudent he would quickly have
the gift of a grave.   30

Sir Toby Belch

By this hand, they are scoundrels and substractors[6]
that say so of him. Who are they?

Maria

They that add. Moreover, he's drunk nightly in your
company.

Sir Toby Belch

toasts   With drinking healths° to my niece. I'll drink to her as   35
long as there is a passage in my throat and drink in
Illyria. He's a coward and a coistrel[7] that will not drink
to my niece till his brains turn o' th' toe like a parish
top.[8] What, wench! *Castiliano vulgo,*[9] for here comes Sir
Andrew Agueface.   40

Enter **Sir Andrew**.

Sir Andrew

Sir Toby Belch! How now, Sir Toby Belch?

1   *shrew*

    Sir Andrew may be confusing the
    word *shrew* with "mouse." A *shrew*
    is, like a mouse, a small rodent,
    but it is also a popular epithet for a
    mean-spirited woman. "Mouse,"
    on the other hand, was sometimes
    used as a term of endearment for
    women; see 1.5.58–59.

2   *Accost*

    I.e., greet; address. From the
    nautical term meaning "pull
    alongside"

3   *"Accost" is front her, board her, woo her,
    assail her.*

    Front, board, and *assail* are all naval
    terms; Sir Toby urges Sir Andrew to
    woo Maria aggressively, like a ship
    might attack an enemy vessel.

4   *undertake her in this company*

    Take her on in public. Sir Andrew
    means that he won't speak to
    Maria publically, but the phrase
    includes an obvious sexual
    innuendo.

5   *An thou let part so*

    If you let her leave in this way (i.e.,
    without speaking to her)

6   *never draw sword again*

    I.e., never again be considered a
    gentleman, with an added sexual
    implication in the word *sword*
    (i.e., penis)

7   *in hand*

    To deal with

Sir Toby Belch

Sweet Sir Andrew!

Sir Andrew

[*to* **Maria**] Bless you, fair shrew. [1]

Maria

And you too, sir.

Sir Toby Belch

Accost, [2] Sir Andrew; accost.   45

Sir Andrew

What's that?

Sir Toby Belch

My niece's chambermaid.

Sir Andrew

Good Mistress Accost, I desire better acquaintance.

Maria

My name is Mary, sir.

Sir Andrew

Good Mistress Mary Accost—   50

Sir Toby Belch

You mistake, knight. "Accost" is front her, board her,
woo her, assail her. [3]

Sir Andrew

By my troth, I would not undertake her in this
company. [4] Is that the meaning of "accost"?

Maria

Fare you well, gentlemen. [*She starts to exit.*]   55

Sir Toby Belch

An thou let part so, [5] Sir Andrew, would thou mightst
never draw sword again. [6]

Sir Andrew

If An° you part so, mistress, I would I might never draw
sword again. Fair lady, do you think you have fools in
hand? [7]   60

1   *thought is free*

    A proverbial expression meaning "one can think whatever one wants," and often used as a response to the question "Do you think I'm a fool?"

2   *buttery-bar*

    The ledge of the door to a buttery, or wine cellar, where drinks were served

3   *What's your metaphor?*

    Most likely, Maria's *metaphor* relies on the comparison of her breasts (or perhaps her backside) to a buttery-bar, upon which Sir Andrew may place his hand. The series of jokes that follow this exchange all feature similar sexual innuendos.

4   *dry*

    Thirsty; dryness was also a sign of old age as well as of a lack of sexual vigor

5   *I am not such an ass but I can keep my hand dry.*

    A play on the old proverb, "Even a fool is smart enough to stay out of the rain."

6   *dry jest*

    (1) a lame joke; (2) a sarcastic joke; (3) a joke about dryness

7   *barren*

    Empty both of jokes and Sir Andrew's hand

8   *canary*

    A sweet wine from the Canary Islands, off the northwest coast of Africa

9   *put down*

    (1) conquered at wordplay; (2) undone by drink (as Sir Andrew uses it in lines 75–76)

10 *beef*

    It was believed that eating too much meat made one dimwitted.

Maria

Sir, I have not you by th' hand.

Sir Andrew

Marry, but you shall have, and here's my hand.

Maria

Now, sir, thought is free.[1] I pray you, bring your hand
to th' buttery-bar[2] and let it drink.

Sir Andrew

Why Wherefore,° sweetheart? What's your metaphor?[3]   65

Maria

It's dry,[4] sir.

Sir Andrew

Why, I think so. I am not such an ass but I can keep my
hand dry.[5] But what's your jest?

Maria

A dry jest,[6] sir.

Sir Andrew

Are you full of them?   70

Maria

Ay, sir, I have them at my fingers' ends. Marry, now I let
go your hand, I am barren.[7]   *Maria exits.*

Sir Toby Belch

O knight, thou lack'st a cup of canary.[8] When did I see
thee so put down?[9]

Sir Andrew

Never in your life, I think, unless you see canary put me   75
down. Methinks sometimes I have no more wit than a
i.e., a regular person Christian° or an ordinary man has. But I am a great
eater of beef,[10] and I believe that does harm to my wit.

Sir Toby Belch

No question.

1 *forswear it*

I.e., give up beef

2 *bear-baiting*

A popular form of entertainment in Shakespeare's day in which packs of dogs attacked chained bears, often taking place in the same amphitheaters used for plays.

3 *by nature*

As opposed to by art. Toby plays on Sir Andrew's admission (line 85) that he had ignored *the arts*.

4 *flax on a distaff*

Flax, a stringy yellow plant, could be turned into thread by spinning its fibers on a *distaff*, a long pole held between the spinner's knees

5 *housewife*

Pronounced "hussif," the word also suggested "hussy," or prostitute. Sir Toby says he wants to see a woman take Sir Andrew between her knees, just as a housewife would take a distaff between hers.

6 *spin it off*

The literal sense is that Sir Andrew's hair will be treated like flax, but the implicit sense is that his hair will fall out when he contracts a venereal disease.

7 *there's life in 't*

There's life in your pursuit; i.e., you still have a chance.

8 *masques and revels*

I.e., pageants and celebrations

Sir Andrew

If An° I thought that, I'd forswear it. [1] I'll ride home   80
tomorrow, Sir Toby.

Sir Toby Belch

Why? (French) *Pourquoi,*° my dear knight?

Sir Andrew

wish What is *pourquoi*? Do or not do? I would° I had bestowed
languages that time in the tongues° that I have in fencing, dancing, and bear-baiting. [2] Oh, had I but followed the arts!   85

Sir Toby Belch

Then hadst thou had an excellent head of hair.

Sir Andrew

improved Why? Would that have mended° my hair?

Sir Toby Belch

Past question, for thou see'st it will not curl by nature. [3]

Sir Andrew

But it becomes me well enough, does 't not?

Sir Toby Belch

Excellent. It hangs like flax on a distaff, [4] and I hope to   90
see a housewife [5] take thee between her legs and spin it
off. [6]

Sir Andrew

Faith, I'll home tomorrow, Sir Toby. Your niece will not
have none be seen. Or if she be, it's four to one she'll none° of me.
near The Count himself, here hard° by, woos her.   95

Sir Toby Belch

She'll none o' th' Count. She'll not match above her
social status / wealth degree,° neither in estate,° years, nor wit. I have heard
her swear 't. Tut, there's life in 't, [7] man.

Sir Andrew

I'll stay a month longer. I am a fellow o' th' strangest
mind i' th' world. I delight in masques and revels [8]   100
sometimes altogether.

1   *kickshawses*

Trifles, worthless things; from the French *quelque chose*, meaning "something"

2   *under the degree of my betters*

I.e., other than those who are my social superiors

3   *galliard*

An energetic, leaping dance step

4   *cut a caper*

I.e., execute a leap; also a pun on *caper*, the pickled condiment that often accompanied mutton dishes (hence Sir Toby's response)

5   *back-trick*

The precise meaning of this phrase is uncertain, though it is one of the capers Sir Andrew boasts of, probably a complicated back kick or backward leap.

6   *curtain*

Often hung over paintings to keep them clean

7   *like to take dust*

Likely to get dusty

8   *Mistress Mall's picture*

Mall, or *Molly*, is a nickname for Mary; it is unclear if *Mistress Mall* refers to a specific woman, though it has been suggested this is a topical reference to Mary Futton, one of the Queen's ladies-in-waiting, involved in a notorious scandal with the Earl of Pembroke in 1601.

9   *coranto*

Another energetic dance step, wilder than the galliard

10   *sink-a-pace*

From the French *cinque pace*, or "five-steps," and another name for the galliard. Sir Toby's pun is on *sink*, the vessel into which one would *make water*.

11   *it was formed under the star of a galliard*

I.e., that you were born in astrological conditions auspicious for dancers

12   *damned colored stock*

"Damned colored stocking" (with *damned* presumably being used as an intensifier). Some editors, assuming the Folio's "damned" to be a misprint, replace the word with "dun" (a dull, brownish gray color). Other critics argue that "damned colored" should be "lemon colored," which would anticipate the yellow stockings Malvolio wears in Act Three, scene four; or perhaps an error for "flame colored."

13   *Taurus*

The sign of the bull. It was believed that each astrological sign ruled specific body parts; traditionally Taurus was said to rule the neck and throat, making it the appropriate sign for a drunkard.

Sir Toby Belch

Art thou good at these kickshawses, [1] knight?

Sir Andrew

As any man in Illyria, whatsoever he be, under the
degree of my betters, [2] and yet I will not compare with
experienced   an old° man.   105

Sir Toby Belch

What is thy excellence in a galliard, [3] knight?

Sir Andrew

Faith, I can cut a caper. [4]

Sir Toby Belch

And I can cut the mutton to 't.

Sir Andrew

And I think I have the back-trick [5] simply as strong as
any man in Illyria.   110

Sir Toby Belch

Why   Wherefore° are these things hid? Wherefore have these
gifts a curtain [6] before 'em? Are they like to take dust, [7]
like Mistress Mall's picture? [8] Why dost thou not go to
church in a galliard and come home in a coranto? [9] My
very walk should be a jig. I would not so much as make   115
urine   water° but in a sink-a-pace. [10] What dost thou mean? Is
talents   it a world to hide virtues° in? I did think, by the excellent constitution of thy leg, it was formed under the
star of a galliard. [11]

Sir Andrew

reasonably   Ay, 'tis strong, and it does indifferent° well in a damned   120
colored stock. [12] Shall we set about some revels?

Sir Toby Belch

What shall we do else? Were we not born under
Taurus? [13]

Sir Andrew

That rules the Taurus! That's° sides and heart.

Sir Toby Belch

rules the No, sir, it is° legs and thighs. Let me see the caper. 125
[*Sir Andrew dances.*] Ha, higher! Ha, ha, excellent!

They exit.

1   *On your attendance*

    At your service

2   *no less but all*

    I.e., everything

3   *address thy gait*

    Direct your steps

4   *thy fixèd foot shall grow*

    **Your unmoving foot will set down
    roots.**

Act 1, Scene 4

*Enter **Valentine** and **Viola** [as Cesario] in men's attire.*

Valentine

kindnesses If the Duke continue these favors° towards you, Cesario,
promoted you are like to be much advanced.° He hath known you
only but° three days, and already you are no stranger.

Viola

moodiness You either fear his humor° or my negligence that you
call in question the continuance of his love. Is he   5
inconstant, sir, in his favors?

Valentine

No, believe me.

*Enter Duke [**Orsino**], **Curio**, and attendants.*

Viola

I thank you. Here comes the Count.

Orsino

Who saw Cesario, ho?

Viola

On your attendance, [1] my lord, here.   10

Orsino

aside [to **Curio** and attendants] Stand you a while aloof.°
[to **Viola**] Cesario,
Thou know'st no less but all. [2] I have unclasped
To thee the book even of my secret soul.
Therefore, good youth, address thy gait [3] unto her;
Be not denied access, stand at her doors,   15
And tell them there thy fixèd foot shall grow [4]
Till thou have audience.

Viola

                              Sure, my noble lord,

1   *leap all civil bounds*

    Disregard the usual niceties

2   *It shall become thee well to act my woes.*

    **It will be appropriate for you to be
    the representative of my desires.**

3   *Diana's*

    **Belonging to Diana, the Roman
    goddess of youth and chastity**

4   *shrill and sound*

    **High in pitch and not yet begun to
    crack or change**

5   *part*

    **Organ or member; but must also
    carry its theatrical sense, especially
    as, in Shakespeare's time, a boy
    actor would have played the
    "woman's part."**

6   *constellation*

    **Character and talents, as
    influenced by the stars**

7   *least in company*

    **Solitude was a hallmark of the
    lover**

8   *Yet a barful strife*

    **And yet, this will be a difficult
    struggle (*barful* = with many
    barriers).**

If she be so abandoned to her sorrow

As it is spoke, she never will admit me.

Orsino

loud; insistent   Be clamorous° and leap all civil bounds [1]   20

unsuccessful   Rather than make unprofited° return.

Viola

Say I do speak with her, my lord; what then?

Orsino

relate   Oh, then unfold° the passion of my love;

genuine   Surprise her with discourse of my dear° faith.

suit   It shall become° thee well to act my woes. [2]   25

She will attend it better in thy youth

messenger's / appearance   Than in a nuncio's° of more grave aspect.°

Viola

I think not so, my lord.

Orsino

                              Dear lad, believe it,

For they shall yet belie thy happy years

That say thou art a man. Diana's [3] lip   30

ruby colored / voice   Is not more smooth and rubious.° Thy small pipe°

Is as the maiden's organ, shrill and sound, [4]

like   And all is semblative° a woman's part. [5]

I know thy constellation [6] is right apt

For this affair. [*to* **Curio** *and attendants*] Some four or five

    attend him.   35

All, if you will, for I myself am best

When least in company. [7] [*to* **Viola**] Prosper well in this,

lavishly   And thou shalt live as freely° as thy lord,

To call his fortunes thine.

Viola

                              I'll do my best

To woo your lady. [*aside*] Yet a barful strife: [8]   40

Whoe'er I woo, myself would be his wife.   *They exit.*

1 *bristle*

A stiff hair, as on a brush

2 *well hanged*

Executed by a hangman, with an added sexual pun on "well hung"

3 *needs to fear no colors*

A proverbial expression meaning "has nothing to fear." Feste also puns on the word "collars," meaning "nooses"—a man who has already been hanged needs not fear nooses any longer.

4 *Make that good.*

Explain what you mean.

5 *lenten*

I.e., thin or meager, like the food many Christians eat during the Lent fasts

6 *In the wars*

Colors (line 9) could also be used in a military sense to mean "flags or banners."

7 *In the wars, and that may you be bold to say in your foolery.*

(1) you're brave enough to make jokes about the war, but too much of a coward to actually fight in one; (2) you might escape punishment by saying you were off in the wars; (3) you would be bold to say you "fear no colors" when you're actually "in the wars" with Lady Olivia, who will be angry at his absence.

8 *talents*

In the New Testament's parable of the talents, Matthew suggests that people should make the most of their God-given gifts (25:13–30).

9 *turned away*

Dismissed

10 *Many a good hanging prevents a bad marriage*

(1) it's better to be dead than badly married; (2) being physically well endowed makes for good sexual relations

11 *bear it out*

Make it tolerable (by virtue of the good weather)

Act 1, Scene 5

Enter **Maria** *and* [**Feste**, *the*] *Clown.*

Maria

by
Nay, either tell me where thou hast been, or I will not open my lips so wide as a bristle[1] may enter in° way of thy excuse. My lady will hang thee for thy absence.

Feste

Let her hang me. He that is well hanged[2] in this world needs to fear no colors.[3]   5

Maria

Make that good.[4]

Feste

He shall see none to fear.

Maria

A good lenten[5] answer. I can tell thee where that saying was born, of "I fear no colors."

Feste

Where, good Mistress Mary?   10

Maria

i.e., that answer
In the wars,[6] and that° may you be bold to say in your foolery.[7]

Feste

Well, God give them wisdom that have it, and those that are fools, let them use their talents.[8]

Maria

Yet you will be hanged for being so long absent, or to   15
be turned away[9]— is not that as good as a hanging to you?

Feste

Many a good hanging prevents a bad marriage,[10] and, for turning away, let summer bear it out.[11]

1 *points*

   Issues; but also the laces used to
   secure a man's trousers.

2 *gaskins*

   Wide knee-length breeches

3 *go thy way*

   I.e., good luck to you

4 *you were best*

   I.e., if you know what's good for you

5 *Quinapalus*

   A made-up name, cited by Feste as
   a parody of learned discourse. In
   productions, Feste often pauses
   after the question, waiting for an
   answer from the audience, and
   then delivers the next sentence as
   if it were a well-known quotation.

6 *Go to*

   An expression of disapproval,
   impatience or disbelief; similar to
   modern expressions like "Get out of
   here" or "Come on, now"

7 *dry*

   Dull, stale. Feste, in reply, also
   puns on the word's other meaning,
   "dehydrated or thirsty."

Maria

You are resolute, then?   20

Feste

Not so, neither, but I am resolved on two points. [1]

Maria

That if one break, the other will hold, or, if both break,
your gaskins [2] fall?

Feste

Apt, in good faith, very apt. Well, go thy way. [3] If Sir

clever   Toby would leave drinking, thou wert as witty° a piece   25

i.e., woman's   of Eve's° flesh as any in Illyria.

Maria

Peace, you rogue; no more o' that. Here comes my
lady. Make your excuse wisely, you were best. [4]

                                              [*She exits.*]

Feste

Intellect / if   [*aside*] Wit,° an° 't be thy will, put me into good fooling!
Those wits that think they have thee do very oft prove   30
fools, and I, that am sure I lack thee, may pass for a
wise man. For what says Quinapalus? [5] "Better a witty
fool than a foolish wit."

              Enter Lady **Olivia** *with* **Malvolio** [*and attendants.*]

                                   ⁴ᴰ Steword

God bless thee, lady!

Olivia

Take the fool away.   35

Feste

Do you not hear, fellows? Take away the lady.

Olivia

Go to, [6] you're a dry [7] fool. I'll no more of you. Besides,
unreliable   you grow dishonest.°

1 *As there is no true cuckold but calamity,*
   so beauty's a flower.

   By vowing to abjure *the sight / And*
   company of men (1.2.36–37),
   following the death of her brother,
   Olivia has in a sense married
   calamity, or sadness. Feste,
   however, says one so "wedded" is
   always—and should always be—
   unfaithful. One can't mourn
   forever, and since beauty fades,
   like *a flower*, Olivia should be
   looking for a husband now. In
   other words, "Give up this life of
   grief before it's too late."

2 *Misprision*

   Misunderstanding (but Feste plays
   homonymically as if it means an
   unjustified arrest)

3 Cucullus non facit monachum

   The hood doesn't make the monk;
   i.e., clothes don't make the man.

4 *I wear not motley in my brain*

   My brain doesn't wear the outfit of
   a fool (i.e., I'm not feeble minded)

5 *catechize*

   Cross-examine, as in Catholic
   religious training

6 *Good my mouse of virtue*

   My good, virtuous mouse. *Mouse*
   was a term of endearment for
   women; see 1.3.43 and note.

Feste

my lady   Two faults, madonna,° that drink and good counsel
will amend. For give the dry fool drink, then is the fool   40
reform   not dry. Bid the dishonest man mend° himself: if he
mend, he is no longer dishonest; if he cannot, let the
tailor   botcher° mend him. Anything that's mended is but
patched. Virtue that transgresses is but patched with
sin, and sin that amends is but patched with virtue. If   45
that this simple syllogism will serve, so. If it will not,
what remedy? As there is no true cuckold but calamity,
ordered   so beauty's a flower.[1] The lady bade° take away the fool;
therefore, I say again, take her away.

Olivia

Sir, I bade them take away you.   50

Feste

Misprision[2] in the highest degree! Lady, *Cucullus non facit
monachum*[3]—that's as much to say as I wear not motley
permission   in my brain.[4] Good madonna, give me leave° to prove
you a fool.

Olivia

Can you do it?   55

Feste

Dexterously, good madonna.

Olivia

Make your proof.

Feste

I must catechize[5] you for it, madonna. Good my mouse
of virtue,[6] answer me.

Olivia

pastime / wait for   Well, sir, for want of other idleness° I'll bide° your   60
proof.

Feste

Good madonna, why mourn'st thou?

1   *mend*

Improve. Olivia means that Feste
has grown smarter or perhaps
more amusing; Malvolio replies
that the clown has indeed
improved, in the sense of "grown
increasingly foolish."

2   *make the better fool*

Make a fool even more foolish

3   *two pence*

Would have been pronounced
"tuppence"

4   *ordinary fool*

(1) untalented jester; (2) jester at an
ordinary, or pub

5   *out of his guard*

Defenseless (an image from
fencing)

6   *minister occasion*

Provide opportunity

7   *set*

Scripted and rehearsed, as
opposed to spontaneous.

8   *zanies*

Assistants, straight men; from
Zanni, the name of a servant
character from the Italian comic
theater known as *commedia dell'arte*.

Olivia

Good fool, for my brother's death.

Feste

I think his soul is in Hell, madonna.

Olivia

I know his soul is in Heaven, fool.   65

Feste

The more fool, madonna, to mourn for your brother's
soul, being in Heaven.—Take away the fool, gentlemen.

Olivia

What think you of this fool, Malvolio? Doth he not
mend?[1]

Malvolio

Yes, and shall do till the pangs of death shake him.   70
Infirmity, that decays the wise, doth ever make the
better fool.[2]

Feste

God send you, sir, a speedy infirmity, for the better
foolishness   increasing your folly!° Sir Toby will be sworn that I am
cunning person / pledge no fox,° but he will not pass° his word for two pence[3]   75
that you are no fool.

Olivia

How say you to that, Malvolio?

Malvolio

dull   I marvel your Ladyship takes delight in such a barren°
by   rascal. I saw him put down the other day with° an ordinary fool[4] that has no more brain than a stone. Look   80
you now, he's out of his guard[5] already. Unless you
silent   laugh and minister occasion[6] to him, he is gagged.° I
laugh   protest I take these wise men that crow° so at these set[7]
kind of fools no better than the fools' zanies.[8]

1 *bird-bolts*

   **Small, blunted arrows used for
   shooting at birds**

2 *rail*

   Speak abusively

3 *Now Mercury endue thee with leasing*

   **May Mercury (the Roman god of
   deceit) give you the gift of lying
   skillfully.**

Olivia

with
out of balance; sick
openhearted

authorized

Oh, you are sick of° self-love, Malvolio, and taste with a   85
distempered° appetite. To be generous, guiltless, and
of free° disposition is to take those things for bird-bolts [1]
that you deem cannon-bullets. There is no slander in
an allowed° fool, though he do nothing but rail, [2] nor
no railing in a known discreet man, though he do   90
nothing but reprove.

Feste

Now Mercury endue thee with leasing, [3] for thou
speak'st well of fools!

Enter **Maria**.

Maria

Madam, there is at the gate a young gentleman much
desires to speak with you.   95

Olivia

From the Count Orsino, is it?

Maria

I know not, madam. 'Tis a fair young man, and well
attended.

Olivia

Who of my people hold him in delay?

Maria

Sir Toby, madam, your kinsman.   100

Olivia

Call
nonsense

Fetch° him off, I pray you. He speaks nothing but
madman.° Fie on him!   [**Maria** *exits.*]
Go you, Malvolio. If it be a suit from the Count, I am
sick or not at home. What you will to dismiss it.

                                        Malvolio *exits.*

1   pia mater

    **I.e., brain (though in actuality the
    Latin name of the membrane that
    surrounds it)**

2   *A plague o' these pickle herring!*

    **Sir Toby presumably belches here
    and blames it on pickled herring
    rather than inebriation.**

3   *Give me faith, say I.*

    **Because faith alone should be
    enough to achieve salvation (and
    defeat the devil) according to
    Protestant belief**

Now you see, sir, how your fooling grows old and   105
people dislike it.

Feste

Thou hast spoke for us, madonna, as if thy eldest son
should be a fool, whose skull Jove cram with brains,
for—here he comes—one of thy kin has a most weak
pia mater. [1]   110

                 Enter **Sir Toby** [**Belch**].

Olivia

By mine honor, half-drunk! What is he at the gate,
cousin?

Sir Toby Belch

A gentleman.

Olivia

A gentleman? What gentleman?

Sir Toby Belch

'Tis a gentleman here—[*He belches.*] A plague o' these   115
drunkard   pickle herring! [2]—How now, sot!°

Feste

Good Sir Toby!

Olivia

Cousin, cousin, how have you come so early by this
lethargy?

Sir Toby Belch

i.e., someone   Lechery? I defy lechery. There's one° at the gate.   120

Olivia

Ay, marry, what is he?

Sir Toby Belch

if   Let him be the devil an° he will; I care not. Give me
the same to me   faith, say I. [3] Well, it's all one.°   *He exits.*

1   *One draught above heat*

    One drink more than the amount needed to keep him warm

2   *drowns him*

    I.e., renders him insensible

3   *let him sit o' my coz*

    Have him hold an inquest for my cousin (i.e., kinsman, Sir Toby).

4   *a sheriff's post*

    Decorative post used to identify the house of the sheriff

Olivia

What's a drunken man like, fool?

Feste

Like a drowned man, a fool, and a madman. One   125
draught above heat[1] makes him a fool, the second
enrages   mads° him, and a third drowns him.[2]

Olivia

coroner   Go thou and seek the crowner,° and let him sit o' my
coz.[3] For he's in the third degree of drink: he's
drowned. Go look after him.   130

Feste

He is but mad yet, madonna, and the fool shall look to
the madman.   [*He exits.*]

Enter **Malvolio**.

Malvolio

Madam, yond young fellow swears he will speak with
you. I told him you were sick. He takes on him to
for that reason   understand so much, and therefore° comes to speak   135
with you. I told him you were asleep. He seems to have
a foreknowledge of that too, and therefore comes to
speak with you. What is to be said to him, lady? He's
fortified against any denial.

Olivia

Tell him he shall not speak with me.   140

Malvolio

He has   H'as° been told so, and he says he'll stand at your door
prop   like a sheriff's post[4] and be the supporter° to a bench,
but he'll speak with you.

Olivia

What kind o' man is he?

1   *in standing water*

    Balanced between high and low tide

2   *shrewishly*

    Usually means "sharply" but here
    may merely mean "in a high pitch"

Malvolio

i.e., ordinary Why, of mankind.° 145

Olivia

What manner of man?

Malvolio

Of very ill manner. He'll speak with you, will you or no.

Olivia

appearance Of what personage° and years is he?

Malvolio

Not yet old enough for a man, nor young enough

unripe peapod / peapod for a boy, as a squash° is before 'tis a peascod,° or a 150

unripe apple codling° when 'tis almost an apple. 'Tis with him in

standing water,[1] between boy and man. He is very

handsome well-favored,° and he speaks very shrewishly.[2] One

scarcely would think his mother's milk were scarce° out of him.

Olivia

Let him approach. Call in my gentlewoman. 155

Malvolio

Gentlewoman, my lady calls. *He exits.*

Enter **Maria**.

Olivia

Give me my veil. Come; throw it o'er my face.

message We'll once more hear Orsino's embassy.°

Enter **Viola**.

Viola

The honorable lady of the house, which is she?

Olivia

Speak to me. I shall answer for her. Your will? 160

1   *comptable*

    Accountable (i.e., sensitive)

2   *least sinister usage*

    I.e., the slightest ill-treatment

3   *studied*

    **Memorized in advance (like lines
    in a play)**

4   *out of my part*

    Not within my scripted role

5   *my profound heart*

    I.e., on my honor

6   *by the very fangs of malice I swear*

    I.e., I swear on my peril.

7   *usurp*

    **Pretend to be; counterfeit. Viola
    takes the word to mean
    "overthrow."**

8   *from my commission*

    **Outside the scope of what I've
    been ordered to say**

9   *forgive you*

    Excuse you from having to deliver

Viola

Most radiant, exquisite, and unmatchable beauty—I
pray you, tell me if this be the lady of the house, for I
never saw her. I would be loath to cast away my speech,
for, besides that it is excellently well penned, I have
memorize taken great pains to con° it. Good beauties, let me   165
suffer sustain° no scorn. I am very comptable,[1] even to the
least sinister usage.[2]

Olivia

Whence came you, sir?

Viola

I can say little more than I have studied,[3] and that question's out of my part.[4] Good gentle one, give me   170
sufficient modest° assurance if you be the lady of the house, that
I may proceed in my speech.

Olivia

actor Are you a comedian?°

Viola

No, my profound heart,[5] and yet, by the very fangs of
malice I swear[6] I am not that I play. Are you the lady of   175
the house?

Olivia

If I do not usurp[7] myself, I am.

Viola

Most certain, if you are she, you do usurp yourself, for
withhold what is yours to bestow is not yours to reserve.°
go on But this is from my commission.[8] I will on° with my   180
speech in your praise and then show you the heart of
my message.

Olivia

Come to what is important in 't. I forgive you[9] the praise.

Viola

Alas, I took great pains to study it, and 'tis poetical.

1   *allowed your approach rather to wonder*
    at you than to hear you
    Allowed you to approach me so
    that I could marvel at you, not
    listen to you

2   *'Tis not that time of moon with me to*
    make one in so skipping a dialogue.
    I.e., I'm not lunatic enough to be
    having such a ridiculous
    conversation. It was believed that
    the moon exerted influence over
    people's reason and sanity.

3   *hoist sail*
    I.e., raise your sails and sail off

4   *hull*
    To *hull* was to lower a ship's sails and
    drift (usually to wait out a storm).

5   *giant*
    In the medieval romances, great
    ladies were said to employ giants
    as bodyguards. Viola is probably
    joking about Maria's small size (see
    2.5.11 and 3.2.60 and note).

6   *I am a messenger.*
    I.e., I deliver messages in both
    directions.

7   *Speak your office.*
    Deliver the message you have been
    given.

8   *taxation of homage*
    Demand for tribute monies

9   *olive*
    I.e., olive branch, the traditional
    symbol of a peace gesture

10 *my entertainment*
    I.e., the manner in which I've been
    welcomed

11 *divinity*
    Religious discourse

12 *text*
    Quotation (usually from the Bible)
    on which a religious sermon is
    based. Olivia and Viola continue to
    develop the theme of "divinity" in
    the following lines.

Olivia

false; contrived It is the more like to be feigned.° I pray you, keep it in. I 185

impudent heard you were saucy° at my gates and allowed your
approach rather to wonder at you than to hear you.¹ If

not completely / sanity you be not° mad, be gone. If you have reason,° be brief.
'Tis not that time of moon with me to make one in so
skipping a dialogue.² 190

Maria

Will you hoist sail,³ sir? Here lies your way.

Viola

deckhand No, good swabber,° I am to hull⁴ here a little longer.

pacification [*to* **Olivia**] Some mollification° for your giant,⁵ sweet
lady. Tell me your mind; I am a messenger.⁶

Olivia

Surely Sure,° you have some hideous matter to deliver, when 195

preamble the courtesy° of it is so fearful. Speak your office.⁷

Viola

declaration It alone concerns your ear. I bring no overture° of war,
no taxation of homage.⁸ I hold the olive⁹ in my hand.

meaning My words are as full of peace as matter.°

Olivia

Yet you began rudely. What are you? What would you? 200

Viola

The rudeness that hath appeared in me have I learned
from my entertainment.¹⁰ What I am and what I would

virginity are as secret as maidenhead:° to your ears, divinity;¹¹ to
any other's, profanation.

Olivia

Give us the place alone. We will hear this divinity. 205

[**Maria** *exits with attendants.*]

Now, sir, what is your text?¹²

Viola

Most sweet lady—

1 *by the method*

   In the same style

2 *are now out of your text*

   Have changed the subject

3 *this present*

   **I.e., on today's date. Olivia unveils
herself as if she were a painting,
inscribed with the date of its
composition as was customary.**

4 *if God did all*

   **If God is responsible for all of it
(i.e., if it is done without
cosmetics)**

5 *blent*

   **Blended (i.e., artificially colored or
painted)**

6 *'Tis beauty truly blent, whose red and
white / Nature's own sweet and cunning
hand laid on. / Lady, you are the cruel'st
she alive / If you will lead these graces to
the grave / And leave the world no copy.*

   **Viola/Cesario speaks here in the
well-established convention of the
poetic blazon. The blazon was a
popular conceit of Renaissance
erotic poetry, characterized by its
itemized meditations on discrete
body parts. A sonnet could be
written, for instance, in praise of a
mistress's eyes, lips, or breasts.
Such poetry had frequent recourse
to the *carpe diem* motif, the urging
of sexual consummation as a
means to outwit mortality.**

**Shakespeare's first fourteen
sonnets treat this theme. Olivia's
satirical reply to Cesario makes
explicit the commodification of
female beauty inherent in this kind
of poetry, her "inventory" being
the form of a list of goods or (more
morbidly) the contents of a will.**

7 *divers schedules*

   Various inventories

8 *every particle and utensil labeled to my will*

   **I.e., each part and aspect itemized
and attached as to a last will and
testament**

Olivia

comforting   A comfortable° doctrine, and much may be said of it.
Where lies your text?

Viola

In Orsino's bosom.   210

Olivia

In his bosom? In what chapter of his bosom?

Viola

To answer by the method:¹ in the first of his heart.

Olivia

Oh, I have read it. It is heresy. Have you no more to say?

Viola

Good madam, let me see your face.

Olivia

authorization   Have you any commission° from your lord to negotiate   215
with my face? You are now out of your text.² But we will
draw the curtain and show you the picture. [*She removes her
veil.*] Look you, sir, such a one I was this present.³ Is 't not
well done?

Viola

Excellently done, if God did all.⁴   220

Olivia

indelible dye   'Tis in grain,° sir. 'Twill endure wind and weather.

Viola

'Tis beauty truly blent,⁵ whose red and white
skillful   Nature's own sweet and cunning° hand laid on.
woman   Lady, you are the cruel'st she° alive
beautiful features   If you will lead these graces° to the grave   225
And leave the world no copy.⁶

Olivia

Oh, sir, I will not be so hard-hearted. I will give out
divers schedules⁷ of my beauty. It shall be inventoried,
and every particle and utensil labeled to my will:⁸ as,

1   *lids*

    **Eyelids, but also playing on the lids
of the *utensils* (i.e., pots and pans)
previously mentioned**

2   *Could be but recompensed though*

    Ought to be repaid, even if

3   *In voices well divulged*

    Well spoken of

4   *in dimension and the shape of nature*

    I.e., in the form of his body

5   *Make me a willow cabin*

    **I would make myself a shelter out
of willow branches. Willow was a
traditional symbol of unrequited
love.**

6   *loyal cantons of contemnèd love*

    Passionate songs of rejected love

moderately item, two lips indifferent° red; item, two gray eyes, 230
with lids¹ to them; item, one neck, one chin, and so
appraise forth. Were you sent hither to praise° me?

Viola

I see you what you are: you are too proud.
even if But if° you were the devil, you are fair.
My lord and master loves you. Oh, such love 235
Could be but recompensed though² you were crowned
paragon The nonpareil° of beauty.

Olivia

How does he love me?

Viola

copious With adorations, fertile° tears,
With groans that thunder love, with sighs of fire.

Olivia

Your lord does know my mind. I cannot love him. 240
Yet I suppose him virtuous, know him noble,
wealth / honorable Of great estate,° of fresh and stainless° youth,
generous In voices well divulged,³ free,° learned, and valiant,
And in dimension and the shape of nature⁴
graceful A gracious° person. But yet I cannot love him. 245
He might have took his answer long ago.

Viola

with / passion If I did love you in° my master's flame,°
deathlike With such a suff'ring, such a deadly° life,
In your denial I would find no sense.
I would not understand it.

Olivia

Why, what would you? 250

Viola

Make me a willow cabin⁵ at your gate
i.e., Olivia And call upon my soul° within the house;
Write loyal cantons of contemnèd love⁶

1   *Halloo your name to the reverberate hills*

I.e., holler (with a pun on *hallow*, "to bless") your name to the echoing hills. Viola's compelling description of lovelorn behavior invokes the figure of Echo, a character in Ovid's *Metamorphoses*. Echo is a nymph spurned by the vain youth Narcissus, whose beauty is a source of pride and self-involvement—in Arthur Golding's 1567 translation of *Metamorphoses* he possesses "the perfect grace / Of white and red indifferently bepainted in his face." Narcissus is thus a figure for the sterility of self-love, and Echo that of a desperate and unreciprocated loyalty. Before meeting Narcissus, Echo was a garrulous nymph who had been sentenced by the goddess Juno to only ever repeat the phrases of others, and upon Narcissus's rejection she wastes away to a mere voice. Narcissus subsequently falls in love with his own image in a pond, and, failing to recognize the reflection for what it is, dies pining for it. Olivia, too, reaps what she sows, for in her love of Cesario she is doomed to a fruitless yearning similar to Narcissus's (2.2.38: *What thriftless sighs shall poor Olivia breathe!*). The correction of such self-love and its redirection to a suitably external object is in part the work of the play.

2   *babbling gossip of the air*

I.e., the nymph Echo (see line 255 and previous note)

3   *Oh, you should not rest / Between the elements of air and earth, / But you should pity me.*

Anyone who lives under the sky and upon the earth (i.e., no human being) would have to pity me.

4   *fortunes*

Current situation (as a servant)

5   *fee'd post*

Messenger for hire

6   *Love make his heart of flint that you shall love*

May love turn the heart of the man you decide to love to stone

7   *give thee fivefold blazon*

I.e., five times proclaim you a gentleman (*blazon* here means the coat of arms that only a gentleman could display)

8   *the master were the man*

I.e., Orsino were Cesario; *man* here meaning servant

And sing them loud even in the dead of night;
Halloo your name to the reverberate hills [1]   255
And make the babbling gossip of the air [2]
Cry out "Olivia!" Oh, you should not rest
Between the elements of air and earth,
But you should pity me. [3]
Olivia
                              You might do much.
What is your parentage?   260
Viola
social standing   Above my fortunes, [4] yet my state° is well.
I am a gentleman.
Olivia
                         Get you to your lord.
I cannot love him. Let him send no more—
Unless perchance you come to me again
To tell me how he takes it. Fare you well.   265
I thank you for your pains. Spend this for me.

                              [*offers* **Viola** *money*]

Viola
I am no fee'd post, [5] lady. Keep your purse.
My master, not myself, lacks recompense.
whom   Love make his heart of flint that° you shall love, [6]
And let your fervor, like my master's, be   270
Placed in contempt. Farewell, fair cruelty.   *She exits.*
Olivia
"What is your parentage?"
"Above my fortunes, yet my state is well.
I am a gentleman." I'll be sworn thou art:
Thy tongue, thy face, thy limbs, actions, and spirit,   275
Hold on   Do give thee fivefold blazon. [7] Not too fast! Soft,° soft!
Unless the master were the man. [8] How now?
Even so quickly may one catch the plague?

1   *Would I or not*
    Whether I wanted it or not

2   *flatter with*
    Encourage

3   *fear to find / Mine eye too great a*
    flatterer for my mind
    **I.e., afraid that my eyes have
    overestimated Cesario, thereby
    overpowering my reason.**

Methinks I feel this youth's perfections
With an invisible and subtle stealth   280
To creep in at mine eyes. Well, let it be.
—What ho, Malvolio!

Enter **Malvolio**.

Malvolio

                    Here, madam, at your service.
Olivia

irritable   Run after that same peevish° messenger,
Count's   The County's° man. He left this ring behind him,
                Would I or not.¹ Tell him I'll none of it. [*gives ring*]   285
                Desire him not to flatter with² his lord,
                Nor hold him up with hopes. I am not for him.
                If that the youth will come this way tomorrow,
Hurry   I'll give him reasons for 't. Hie° thee, Malvolio.
Malvolio

                Madam, I will.   *He exits.*   290
Olivia

                I do I know not what and fear to find
                Mine eye too great a flatterer for my mind.³
own; control   Fate, show thy force. Ourselves we do not owe.°
                What is decreed must be, and be this so.   [*She exits.*]

1   *will you not*
    Do you not wish

2   *The malignancy of my fate might*
    perhaps distemper yours
    The maliciousness of the stars'
    influence over my fate might
    perhaps harm yours, as well

3   *My determinate voyage is mere*
    extravagancy.
    I.e., I only intend to wander.

4   *you will not extort from me what I am*
    willing to keep in
    You will not force me to say that
    which I'd rather not reveal

5   *it charges me in manners*
    I.e., good manners require me

6   *to express myself*
    To reveal who I am

7   *You must know of me then, Antonio: My*
    name is Sebastian, which I called Roderigo.
    The indication of an alias is
    nowhere else referred to, perhaps
    suggesting a plotline left
    undeveloped. Sebastian's
    disclosure of his identity thus may
    seem clumsy in terms of any
    imagined relationship between
    these men, although it is of
    obvious theatrical practicality, as
    the audience needs to know who
    these men are. The suggestion of
    Sebastian's elusiveness does
    however contribute to the erotic
    dynamic between himself and

Antonio: Sebastian seems to seek a
parting of ways, while Antonio
appears determined to pursue
him. Productions differ with time,
taste, and culture in the degree to
which they make explicit the
homoerotic nature of this
relationship.

8   *Messaline*
    A name apparently invented by
    Shakespeare, perhaps conflating
    Messina (in Sicily) and Mitylene
    (on Lesbos) or perhaps derived
    from the Latin name of the French
    city of Marseilles

9   *an hour*
    I.e., the same hour

10 *some hour*
    About an hour

11 *I could not with such estimable wonder*
    overfar believe that
    I.e., though I cannot vouch for this
    (the fact of Viola's beauty) so
    strongly and enthusiastically
    (because to do so would
    immodestly reflect upon himself)

Act 2, Scene 1

Enter **Antonio** *and* **Sebastian**.

Antonio

Will you stay no longer, nor will you not[1] that I go with
you?

Sebastian

menacingly By your patience, no. My stars shine darkly° over me.
The malignancy of my fate might perhaps distemper
yours;[2] therefore I shall crave of you your leave that I   5
repayment may bear my evils alone. It were a bad recompense° for
your love to lay any of them on you.

Antonio

Let me yet know of you whither you are bound.

Sebastian

truly No, sooth,° sir. My determinate voyage is mere
extravagancy.[3] But I perceive in you so excellent a touch of   10
courtesy modesty° that you will not extort from me what I am
willing to keep in;[4] therefore it charges me in manners[5]
the rather to express myself.[6] You must know of me
then, Antonio: My name is Sebastian, which I called
Roderigo.[7] My father was that Sebastian of Messaline,[8]   15
whom I know you have heard of. He left behind him
myself and a sister, both born in an hour.[9] If the heavens had been pleased, would we had so ended! But you,
sir, altered that, for some hour[10] before you took me
surf from the breach° of the sea was my sister drowned.   20

Antonio

Alas the day!

Sebastian

A lady, sir, though it was said she much resembled me,
was yet of many accounted beautiful. But though I could
not with such estimable wonder overfar believe that,[11]

1 *a mind that envy could not but call fair*

   A mind that even the most envious
   people would have to admit was
   beautiful.

2 *more*

   More salt water (i.e., my tears)

3 *trouble*

   I.e., effort on my behalf

4 *murder me*

   I.e., have me die of grief (by
   insisting that we part)

5 *My bosom is full of kindness*

   My heart is full of tenderness.

6 *so near the manners of my mother*

   I.e., so filled with a woman's
   readiness to weep (See LONGER NOTE,
   page 288.)

7 *mine eyes will tell tales of me*

   I.e., my eyes will betray me

proclaim yet thus far I will boldly publish° her: she bore a mind   25
that envy could not but call fair. [1] She is drowned
already, sir, with salt water, though I seem to drown
her remembrance again with more. [2]

Antonio

reception Pardon me, sir, your bad entertainment.°

Sebastian

O good Antonio, forgive me your trouble. [3]   30

Antonio

If you will not murder me [4] for my love, let me be your
servant.

Sebastian

If you will not undo what you have done—that is, kill
rescued him whom you have recovered°— desire it not. Fare
you well at once. My bosom is full of kindness, [5] and I   35
still am yet° so near the manners of my mother [6] that, upon
the least occasion more, mine eyes will tell tales of
me. [7] I am bound to the Count Orsino's court. Farewell.

He exits.

Antonio

good favor The gentleness° of all the gods go with thee!
I have many enemies in Orsino's court,   40
Or else Else° would I very shortly see thee there.
But come what may, I do adore thee so
That danger shall seem sport, and I will go.   *He exits.*

1   several
    Separate

2   *since arrived but hither*
    Only come this far

3   *desperate assurance*
    Guarantee of hopelessness

4   *this*
    I.e., this message (of rejection)

5   *She took the ring of me.*
    **Viola seems to be improvising a lie
    in order to protect Olivia's
    reputation.**

6   *my outside*
    **My outward appearance (i.e., my
    disguise as a boy)**

7   *made good view of me*
    Carefully scrutinized me

8   *her eyes had lost her tongue*
    **I.e., that the sight (of me) had
    taken away her power of speech**

9   *in starts distractedly*
    Agitatedly, in fits and starts

Act 2, Scene 2

*Enter **Viola** and **Malvolio** at several[1] doors.*

Malvolio

just   Were not you even° now with the Countess Olivia?

Viola

At   Even now, sir. On° a moderate pace I have since arrived
but hither.[2]

Malvolio

   She returns this ring to you, sir. You might have saved
me my pains to have taken it away yourself. She adds,   5
moreover, that you should put your lord into a

have none   desperate assurance[3] she will none° of him. And one

bold as   thing more, that you be never so hardy° to come again
in his affairs, unless it be to report your lord's taking of
this.[4] Receive it so.   10

Viola

   She took the ring of me.[5] I'll none of it.

Malvolio

irritably   Come, sir, you peevishly° threw it to her, and her will is
it should be so returned. [*He drops the ring.*] If it be worth

i.e. sight   stooping for, there it lies in your eye.° If not, be it his
that finds it.   *He exits.*   15

Viola

   [*picking up the ring*] I left no ring with her. What means this
       lady?

captivated   Fortune forbid my outside[6] have not charmed° her!
She made good view of me,[7] indeed so much
That methought her eyes had lost her tongue,[8]
For she did speak in starts distractedly.[9]   20

craftiness   She loves me, sure! The cunning° of her passion

by means of   Invites me in° this churlish messenger.
None of my lord's ring? Why, he sent her none.

1   *the man*

    I.e., the man she loves

2   *pregnant enemy*

    I.e., the devil, the *pregnant*
    (ingenious; resourceful) *enemy* who
    uses deceit and *disguise* to assail
    mankind. "Satan" means "enemy"
    in Hebrew.

3   *proper false*

    Those who are both attractive
    (*proper*) and deceitful (*false*)

4   *In women's waxen hearts to set their*
    forms

    To make their marks on the
    impressionable hearts of women
    (like a seal making an impression
    in wax)

5   *such as we are made of, such we be*

    We can only be like that which we
    are made of (i.e., frail flesh)

6   *monster*

    Because Viola is both woman and
    man

7   *As I am man, / My state is desperate for*
    my master's love

    Viola's love for Orsino will
    continue to be *desperate* (i.e.,
    hopeless) as long as she plays the
    role of a man.

I am the man.[1] If it be so, as 'tis,

Poor lady, she were better love a dream.   25

Disguise, I see thou art a wickedness,

Wherein the pregnant enemy[2] does much.

How easy is it for the proper false[3]

In women's waxen hearts to set their forms![4]

Alas, our frailty is the cause, not we,   30

For such as we are made of, such we be.[5]

turn out   How will this fadge?° My master loves her dearly,

dote   And I, poor monster,[6] fond° as much on him,

And she, mistaken, seems to dote on me.

What will become of this? As I am man,   35

My state is desperate for my master's love;[7]

As I am woman—now, alas the day—

useless   What thriftless° sighs shall poor Olivia breathe!

O time, thou must untangle this, not I.

It is too hard a knot for me t' untie!   [*She exits.*] 40

1   diluculo surgere

The beginning of a Latin proverb (*diluculo surgere saluberrimum est*) meaning, "To get up early is very healthful."

2   *unfilled can*

Empty drinking mug

3   *four elements*

The *four elements* of matter were considered to be fire, air, water, and earth (See LONGER NOTE, page 288.)

4   *stoup*

Tankard holding about two pints of liquid

5   *the picture of "We Three"*

The title of a well-known type of picture, which depicted two fools' or two asses' heads with an inscription "We three," the viewer being, by implication, the third.

6   *catch*

Round; a popular tune sung in multiple parts, such as "Row, Row, Row Your Boat"

Act 2, Scene 3

Enter **Sir Toby [Belch]** *and* **Sir Andrew**.

Sir Toby Belch

Approach, Sir Andrew. Not to be abed after midnight

early is to be up betimes,° and *diluculo surgere*,¹ thou

know'st—

Sir Andrew

faith Nay, by my troth,° I know not, but I know to be up late

is to be up late.   5

Sir Toby Belch

as I hate A false conclusion. I hate it as° an unfilled can.² To be

up after midnight and to go to bed then is early, so that

to go to bed after midnight is to go to bed betimes.

Does not our life consist of the four elements?³

Sir Andrew

Faith, so they say, but I think it rather consists of eating   10

and drinking.

Sir Toby Belch

Thou 'rt a scholar. Let us therefore eat and drink.

[*calling*] Marian, I say! A stoup⁴ of wine!

*Enter [***Feste***, the] Clown.*

Sir Andrew

Here comes the fool, i' faith.

Feste

How now, my hearts! Did you never see the picture of   15

"We Three"?⁵

Sir Toby Belch

Welcome, ass. Now let's have a catch.⁶

1 *leg*

I.e., talent for dancing

2 *Pigrogromitus, of the Vapians passing the equinoctial of Queubus*

More examples of Feste's fabricated scholarly double-talk

3 *I did impeticos thy gratillity*

More comic nonsense, roughly meaning, "I did impocket (i.e., put in my pocket) your gratuity (i.e., money)"

4 *for Malvolio's nose is no whipstock, my lady has a white hand, and the Myrmidons are no bottle-ale houses*

More of Feste's comic double-talk. The approximate sense is: "Malvolio's nose is not a whip handle, my lady's hand is white (and therefore, according to Elizabethan aesthetics, beautiful), and ancient Greek soldiers, the followers of Achilles, (with a pun on *Mermaid Inn*, the name of an upscale London tavern) are not cheap pubs serving second-rate ale."

5 *testril*

Tester (a coin worth sixpence)

6 *give a—*

The 1623 First Folio prints this line without punctuation, leading some scholars to speculate that, during the printing process, the continuation of Andrew's line was inadvertently dropped. Other scholars argue that this is either a deliberate indication that Feste should cut Sir Andrew off before the knight can launch into some long digression, or that Sir Andrew in his drunkenness simply trails off into silence.

Sir Andrew

i.e., Feste / voice

By my troth, the fool° has an excellent breast.° I had
rather than forty shillings I had such a leg, [1] and so
sweet a breath to sing, as the fool has. [*to* **Feste**] In 20

inspired

sooth, thou wast in very gracious° fooling last night
when thou spok'st of Pigrogromitus, of the Vapians
passing the equinoctial of Queubus. [2] 'Twas very good,

sweetheart

i' faith. I sent thee sixpence for thy leman.° Hadst it?

Feste

I did impeticos thy gratillity, [3] for Malvolio's nose is no 25
whipstock, my lady has a white hand, and the Myrmidons are no bottle-ale houses. [4]

Sir Andrew

Excellent! Why, this is the best fooling when all is
done. Now, a song.

Sir Toby Belch

[*handing money to* **Feste**] Come on. There is sixpence for 30
you. Let's have a song.

Sir Andrew

[*handing money to* **Feste**] There's a testril [5] of me too. If
one knight give a— [6]

Feste

Would you have a love song or a song of good life?

Sir Toby Belch

A love song, a love song. 35

Sir Andrew

Ay, ay. I care not for good life.

Feste

   [*sings*] O mistress mine, where are you roaming?
   Oh, stay and hear! Your true love's coming
   That can sing both high and low.

Travel / darling

   Trip° no further, pretty sweeting.° 40

1   *Every wise man's son*

I.e., every fool. According to a well-known proverb of the time, wise men have foolish sons.

2   *hereafter*

To come (at a future date)

3   *sweet and twenty*

The phrase either gives two descriptions of the lover (who might be both *sweet* and *twenty* years old) or is an intensified form of sweet (twenty times sweet).

4   *contagious breath*

(1) catchy tune; (2) foul-smelling or disease-causing breath

5   *To hear by the nose, it is dulcet*

I.e., if we could hear through our noses, we would consider the sound sweet

6   *welkin*

The sky; the heavens

7   *three souls out of one weaver*

Music was thought to have the power to make the soul rise out of the body. Weavers traditionally sang psalms while working their looms.

8   *By'r lady*

A mild oath, meaning "by the Virgin Mary."

9   *"Thou Knave"*

A popular song in which the singers refer to one another as "thou knave" (i.e., you fool).

10   *"Hold thy peace, thou knave"*

Lyrics from the song

11   *constrained in 't*

Forced (by the lyrics of the song)

>   Journeys end in lovers meeting,
>   Every wise man's son [1] doth know.

Sir Andrew

Excellent good, i' faith.

Sir Toby Belch

Good, good.

Feste

>   [*sings*] What is love? 'Tis not hereafter. [2]   45
>   Present mirth hath present laughter.

always   What's to come is still° unsure.

>   In delay there lies no plenty.
>   Then come kiss me, sweet and twenty. [3]
>   Youth's a stuff will not endure.   50

Sir Andrew

A mellifluous voice, as I am true knight.

Sir Toby Belch

A contagious breath. [4]

Sir Andrew

Very sweet and contagious, i' faith.

Sir Toby Belch

To hear by the nose, it is dulcet [5] in contagion. But shall
we make the welkin [6] dance indeed? Shall we rouse the   55
night owl in a catch that will draw three souls out of
one weaver? [7] Shall we do that?

Sir Andrew

i.e., If/skilled   An° you love me, let's do 't. I am dog° at a catch.

Feste

By 'r lady, [8] sir, and some dogs will catch well.

Sir Andrew

Most certain. Let our catch be "Thou Knave." [9]   60

Feste

"Hold thy peace, thou knave," [10] knight? I shall be constrained in 't [11] to call thee "knave," knight.

1   *caterwauling*

A noise like fighting cats.

2   *Cathayan*

The exact meaning of this phrase is
contested. *Cathay* was the name
given to North China by medieval
Europeans, so *Cathayan* could mean
"Chinese person"—and by
extension, according to English
beliefs of the time, someone who
was untrustworthy. The phrase,
however, could also refer to those
European explorers who traveled
to China and fraudulently boasted
of the riches they discovered there.
In either case, Toby is assuming
that Olivia will not throw him out,
as Maria just warned.

3   *Peg-a-Ramsey*

The flirtatious title character of a
popular song (meant as an insult to
Malvolio).

4   *Three merry men be we*

A refrain from another popular song.

5   *consanguineous*

Of the same blood (i.e., related to
Olivia)

6   *Tilly-vally*

A nonsense term used to express
dismissal, impatience, or disdain.

7   *There dwelt a man in Babylon, lady, lady!*

The first line of a popular ballad
based on the biblical story of
Susanna and the Elders.

8   *more natural*

Naturally, easily (with a pun on
"more like a *natural*," or "more like
an imbecile")

9   *O' the twelfth day of December*

Another line from a popular song.

Sir Andrew

someone   'Tis not the first time I have constrained one° to call me
"knave." Begin, fool. It begins "Hold thy peace."

Feste

I shall never begin if I hold my peace.   65

Sir Andrew

Good, i' faith. Come, begin.   *Catch sung.*

Enter **Maria**.

Maria

What a caterwauling[1] do you keep here! If my lady have
not called up her steward Malvolio and bid him turn
you out of doors, never trust me.

Sir Toby Belch

i.e., schemers   My lady's a Cathayan.[2] We are politicians,° Malvolio's a   70
Peg-a-Ramsey,[3] and [*sings*] Three merry men be we.[4]—
Am not I consanguineous?[5] Am I not of her blood?
Tilly-vally![6] "Lady"! [*sings*] There dwelt a man in Baby-
lon, lady, lady![7]

Feste

Curse   Beshrew° me, the knight's in admirable fooling.   75

Sir Andrew

Ay, he does well enough if he be disposed, and so do I
too. He does it with a better grace, but I do it more
natural.[8]

Sir Toby Belch

    [*sings*] O' the twelfth day of December[9]—

Maria

For the love o' God, peace!   80

Enter **Malvolio**.

1 *gabble like tinkers*

Talk gibberish like itinerant
menders of household goods.
Tinkers were thought of as heavy
drinkers who spoke nonsense
when drunk.

2 *coziers' catches*

Shoemakers' tunes. Shoemakers,
like the other workingmen
mentioned in the scene (i.e.,
tinkers and weavers), traditionally
sang on the job.

3 *mitigation or remorse of voice*

I.e., softening or lessening of
volume

4 *though she harbors you as her kinsman,*
   she's nothing allied to your disorders

I.e., though she keeps you in her
house since you are a relative, she
is in no way related to your
disorderly conduct.

5 *Farewell, dear heart, since I must needs*
   be gone.

A line from a well-known love
ballad in which a dying lover frets
about leaving his beloved. In the
following lines, Toby, Andrew, and
Feste ironically adapt the lyrics to
irritate Malvolio.

Malvolio

My masters, are you mad? Or what are you? Have you
sense / propriety no wit,° manners, nor honesty° but to gabble like
tinkers¹ at this time of night? Do you make an ale-
house of my lady's house, that you squeak out your
coziers' catches² without any mitigation or remorse of   85
voice?³ Is there no respect of place, persons, nor time
in you?

Sir Toby Belch

songs / Shut We did keep time, sir, in our catches.° Sneck° up!

Malvolio

blunt Sir Toby, I must be round° with you. My lady bade me
tell you that, though she harbors you as her kinsman,   90
she's nothing allied to your disorders.⁴ If you can separate yourself and your misdemeanors, you are wel-
if come to the house. If not, an° it would please you to
take leave of her, she is very willing to bid you farewell.

Sir Toby Belch

[*sings*] Farewell, dear heart, since I must needs be gone.⁵ 95

Maria

Nay, good Sir Toby.

Feste

[*sings*] His eyes do show his days are almost done.

Malvolio

Is 't even so?

Sir Toby Belch

[*sings*] But I will never die.

Feste

[*sings*] Sir Toby, there you lie.   100

Malvolio

This is much credit to you.

Sir Toby Belch

[*sings*] Shall I bid him go?

1 *Art any more than a steward?*

The *steward* was chief servant of a household, responsible for the behavior of lesser servants, although fools and ladies-in-waiting were probably out of his purview. He was responsible, perhaps, for the dispensing of provisions such as *cakes and ale*, and so one of the sources of Sir Toby's resentment toward Malvolio may be the latter's possession of the cellar keys. Sir Toby's question is an attempt to pull rank, reminding Malvolio of his low birth and mocking the latter's conviction that proper behavior has anything to do with status. Malvolio is here in the difficult position of regulating the behavior of his social betters; he is appalled not only at their indecorous failure to *respect* neither *place, persons, nor time* (2.3.86)—Olivia's house, Olivia and other sleeping persons, the time of night—but perhaps also at their failure to behave in a manner fitting their noble rank.

2 *cakes and ale*

I.e, celebrations. Cake and ale were traditionally served and consumed during church festivals (and so disliked by Puritans).

3 *Saint Anne*

The mother of the Virgin Mary; she was a favorite in Catholic popular religion and so a focus of Puritan disdain.

4 *ginger*

Root used to spice ale

5 *rub your chain with crumbs*

Clean your steward's chain (i.e., get out of here and remember who you are)

6 *by this hand*

I.e., on my word

7 *Go shake your ears!*

Asses typically shake their ears; the phrase has the general sense of "Get lost, you ass."

8 *'Twere as good a deed as to drink when a man's a-hungry*

As good a deed as to drink was a proverbial phrase roughly meaning, "It's always the right thing to do"; Sir Andrew's addition makes nonsense of the sentence.

9 *the field*

To a duel

Feste

> [*sings*] What an if you do?

Sir Toby Belch

> [*sings*] Shall I bid him go, and spare not?

Feste

> [*sings*] Oh no, no, no, no, you dare not.   105

Sir Toby Belch

Out o' tune, sir. Ye lie. Art any more than a steward?[1]
Dost thou think because thou art virtuous there shall
be no more cakes and ale?[2]

Feste

Yes, by Saint Anne,[3] and ginger[4] shall be hot i' th'
mouth too.   110

Sir Toby Belch

Thou 'rt i' th' right. Go, sir, rub your chain with
crumbs.[5] A stoup of wine, Maria!

Malvolio

Mistress Mary, if you prized my lady's favor at anything
more than contempt, you would not give means for°   *to enable*
this uncivil rule.° She shall know of it, by this hand.[6]   115   *conduct*

> *He exits.*

Maria

Go shake your ears![7]

Sir Andrew

'Twere as good a deed as to drink when a man's a-hungry,[8]
to challenge him the field[9] and then to break promise
with him and make a fool of him.

Sir Toby Belch

Do 't, knight. I'll write thee a challenge, or I'll deliver   120
thy indignation to him by word of mouth.

Maria

Sweet Sir Toby, be patient for tonight. Since the youth
of the Count's was today with my lady, she is much

1 *gull him into a nayword*
Trick him into becoming a byword, i.e., make him notorious (for stupidity)

2 *sometimes he is kind of puritan*
Puritan was a blanket term for any number of religious sectarians dissatisfied with the extent to which England's national church had reformed itself in order to distance itself from the practices of Roman Catholicism. Puritans were known for their general hostility toward festivity: bear-baiting (cf. 2.5.7), the public theater, and religious holiday celebrations were among the particular targets of their dislike. (See LONGER NOTE, page 288.)

3 *The devil a puritan that he is, or anything constantly but a time-pleaser*
He's not really a puritan; he's not anything consistently, except a flatterer

4 *cons state without book and utters it by great swaths*
Memorizes important sounding language and then parrots back great portions of it

5 *the best persuaded of himself*
Holding the highest opinion of himself

6 *grounds of faith*
Fundamental belief

7 *obscure epistles of love*
Disguised love letters

8 *feelingly personated*
Appropriately portrayed

sorts out of quiet.° For Monsieur Malvolio, let me alone with
him. If I do not gull him into a nayword[1] and make him   125
common source of a common° recreation, do not think I have wit enough
to lie straight in my bed. I know I can do it.

Sir Toby Belch

Inform Possess° us; possess us. Tell us something of him.

Maria

Marry, sir, sometimes he is a kind of puritan.[2]

Sir Andrew

Oh, if I thought that, I'd beat him like a dog!   130

Sir Toby Belch

ingenious What? For being a puritan? Thy exquisite° reason, dear
knight?

Sir Andrew

I have no exquisite reason for 't, but I have reason good
enough.

Maria

The devil a puritan that he is, or anything constantly   135
affected but a time-pleaser;[3] an affectioned° ass that cons state
without book and utters it by great swaths;[4] the best
persuaded of himself,[5] so crammed, as he thinks, with
excellencies, that it is his grounds of faith[6] that all that
look on him love him. And on that vice in him will my   140
revenge find notable cause to work.

Sir Toby Belch

What wilt thou do?

Maria

I will drop in his way some obscure epistles of love,[7]
wherein by the color of his beard, the shape of his leg,
expression the manner of his gait, the expressure° of his eye, fore-   145
head, and complexion, he shall find himself most feel-
ingly personated.[8] I can write very like my lady your
niece: on a forgotten matter we can hardly make

1   *Penthesilea*

    Queen of the Amazons, a mythical
    race of warrior women and
    probably an ironic joke about
    Maria's small stature.

2   *Before me*

    A mild oath, a substitution for
    "Before God."

handwriting   distinction of our hands.°

Sir Toby Belch

plot   Excellent! I smell a device.°   150

Sir Andrew

I have 't in my nose too.

Sir Toby Belch

He shall think, by the letters that thou wilt drop, that they come from my niece, and that she's in love with him.

Maria

My purpose is, indeed, a horse of that color.   155

Sir Andrew

And your horse now would make him an ass.

Maria

Ass, I doubt not.

Sir Andrew

Oh, 'twill be admirable!

Maria

medicine   Sport royal, I warrant you. I know my physic° will work

i.e., Feste   with him. I will plant you two—and let the fool° make a   160
third—where he shall find the letter. Observe his

interpretation   construction° of it. For this night, to bed, and dream

outcome   on the event.° Farewell.   *She exits.*

Sir Toby Belch

Good night, Penthesilea.[1]

Sir Andrew

Before me,[2] she's a good wench.   165

Sir Toby Belch

She's a beagle true-bred, and one that adores me. What o' that?

Sir Andrew

I was adored once too.

1   *a foul way out*

   I.e., in deep financial trouble

2   *"Cut"*

   **A term of contempt; literally a
   gelded horse, but also slang for
   female genitalia.**

3   *burn some sack*

   **Heat and spice some sack (Spanish
   white wine)**

Sir Toby Belch

Let's to bed, knight. Thou hadst need send for more
money.   170

Sir Andrew

win   If I cannot recover° your niece, I am a foul way out. [1]

Sir Toby Belch

Send for money, knight. If thou hast her not i' the end,
call me "Cut." [2]

Sir Andrew

If I do not, never trust me, take it how you will.

Sir Toby Belch

Come; come. I'll go burn some sack. [3] 'Tis too late to go   175
to bed now. Come, knight. Come, knight.   *They exit.*

1   *antique*

    Old-fashioned, quaint

2   *recollected terms*

    Unoriginal, fashionable verses

3   *brisk and giddy-pacèd*

    Shallow and fast paced

4   *in all motions else*

    In all other emotions

5   *Save in the constant image of*

    Except for the consistent focus on

6   *It gives a very echo to the seat / Where
    love is throned.*

    **It perfectly reflects the feelings of
    the heart, the place where love sits
    enthroned.**

Act 2, Scene 4

*Enter Duke [**Orsino**], **Viola**, **Curio**, and others.*

Orsino

morning Give me some music. Now, good morrow,° friends.

just —Now, good Cesario, but° that piece of song,

That old and antique¹ song we heard last night.

suffering Methought it did relieve my passion° much,

tunes More than light airs° and recollected terms²   5

Of these most brisk and giddy-pacèd³ times:

just Come, but° one verse.

Curio

He is not here, so please your lordship, that should

sing it.

Orsino

Who was it?   10

Curio

Feste the jester, my lord, a fool that the Lady Olivia's

father took much delight in. He is about the house.

Orsino

Seek him out, [*to musicians*] and play the tune the while.

[**Curio** *exits.*] *Music plays.*

[*to* **Viola**] Come hither, boy. If ever thou shalt love,

In the sweet pangs of it remember me,   15

For such as I am, all true lovers are,

Unsteady / frivolous Unstaid° and skittish° in all motions else⁴

Save in the constant image of⁵ the creature

That is beloved. How dost thou like this tune?

Viola

It gives a very echo to the seat   20

Where love is throned.⁶

Orsino

                              Thou dost speak masterly.°
expertly

1   *stayed upon some favor*

    Fixated on some face

2   *by your favor*

    **By your leave; if you don't mind.
    Viola's phrase is also a pun on *favor*,
    meaning face—she suggests that
    her *eye hath stayed upon* Orsino's
    face and subsequently fallen in
    love with it.**

3   *wears she to him*

    She adapts herself to suit him

4   *sways she level in her husband's heart*

    **I.e., she is steadily loved by her
    husband**

5   *cannot hold the bent*

    **I.e., cannot sustain itself at full
    strength. The phrase *the bent* comes
    from archery: a bow drawn back all
    the way is "at its full bent."**

6   *even when*

    Precisely at the point when

My life upon 't, young though thou art, thine eye
Hath stayed upon some favor¹ that it loves.
Hath it not, boy?

Viola

A little, by your favor.²

Orsino

What kind of woman is 't?

Viola

Of your complexion. 25

Orsino

She is not worth thee, then. What years, i' faith?

Viola

About your years, my lord.

Orsino

always Too old, by Heaven. Let still° the woman take
An elder than herself. So wears she to him;³
So sways she level in her husband's heart.⁴ 30
For, boy, however we do praise ourselves,
affections Our fancies° are more giddy and unfirm,
exhausted More longing, wavering, sooner lost and worn,°
Than women's are.

Viola

believe I think° it well, my lord.

Orsino

Then let thy love be younger than thyself, 35
Or thy affection cannot hold the bent.⁵
For women are as roses, whose fair flower
in bloom Being once displayed,° doth fall that very hour.

Viola

And so they are. Alas that they are so,
To die even when⁶ they to perfection grow! 40

*Enter **Curio** and [**Feste**, the] clown.*

1   *spinsters*

**Women who spin thread on
wheels.**

2   *weave their thread with bones*

**Weave lace on frames made of
bone**

3   *silly sooth*

Simple truth

4   *sad cypress*

**Coffins were often made of cypress
wood.**

5   *yew*

**Sprigs of the yew tree, which were
often found growing in graveyards
and its sprigs strewn over the
corpse.**

6   *My part of death, no one so true / Did
share it.*

**I.e., I am the most faithful lover
who has ever died of unrequited
love.**

Orsino

Oh, fellow, come, the song we had last night.

—Mark it, Cesario, it is old and plain.

The spinsters[1] and the knitters in the sun

carefree And the free° maids that weave their thread with bones[2]

Do use to chant it. It is silly sooth[3] 45

deals And dallies° with the innocence of love

days Like the old age.°

Feste

Are you ready, sir?

Orsino

Ay; prithee, sing. *Music.*

Feste

here [*sings*] Come away,° come away, death, 50

And in sad cypress[4] let me be laid.

Fly away, fly away breath,

I am slain by a fair cruel maid.

My shroud of white, stuck all with yew,[5]

Oh, prepare it! 55

My part of death, no one so true

Did share it.[6]

Not a flower, not a flower sweet

strewn On my black coffin let there be strown.°

Not a friend, not a friend greet 60

My poor corpse, where my bones shall be thrown.

A thousand thousand sighs to save,

Lay me, oh, where

Sad true lover never find my grave

To weep there! 65

Orsino

efforts [*handing him money*] There's for thy pains.°

1   *pleasure will be paid, one time or another*
    I.e., every pleasant thing has its price.

2   *Give me now leave to leave thee.*
    I.e., give me permission to be apart from you (a polite way to dismiss Feste).

3   *the melancholy god*
    Saturn, the Roman god of sadness and melancholy

4   *changeable taffeta*
    I.e., shot silk, a fabric woven in such a way that its color appears to change when seen from different angles.

5   *opal*
    A multicolored, iridescent gemstone.

6   *men of such constancy*
    Men who, like you, are changeable

7   *sea*
    Notorious for being changeable. With the images of *changeable taffeta*, *opals*, and the *sea*, Feste comments upon Orsino's sudden shift from good cheer into melancholy.

8   *for that's it that always makes a good voyage of nothing*
    I.e., for that (being unpredictable; having no specific destination) is a way to make profitable an otherwise pointless trip.

9   *give place*
    Leave

10 *sovereign cruelty*
    Master of cruelty (i.e., Olivia)

11 *quantity of dirty lands*
    Parcels of worthless land (i.e., Olivia's properties)

12 *The parts*
    I.e., the wealth and position

13 *hold as giddily as fortune*
    Value lightly. *Fortune* (luck) is usually depicted as being *giddy* (fickle).

14 *that miracle and queen of gems / That nature pranks her in*
    I.e., her beauty, with which nature has adorned her (*pranks* means "fancily dresses").

Feste

No pains, sir. I take pleasure in singing, sir.

Orsino

I'll pay thy pleasure then.

Feste

paid for   Truly, sir, and pleasure will be paid,° one time or
another. [1]   70

Orsino

Give me now leave to leave thee. [2]

Feste

Now, the melancholy god [3] protect thee, and the tailor
jacket   make thy doublet° of changeable taffeta, [4] for thy mind
is a very opal. [5] I would have men of such constancy [6] put
to sea, [7] that their business might be everything and
destination   their intent° everywhere, for that's it that always makes   75
a good voyage of nothing. [8] Farewell.   *He exits.*

Orsino

Let all the rest give place. [9]

                    [**Curio** *and the attendants exit.*]
                         Once more, Cesario,
Get thee to yond same sovereign cruelty. [10]
Tell her my love, more noble than the world,
Values   Prizes° not quantity of dirty lands. [11]   80
The parts [12] that fortune hath bestowed upon her,
Tell her, I hold as giddily as fortune. [13]
But 'tis that miracle and queen of gems
That nature pranks her in [14] attracts my soul.

Viola   85

But if she cannot love you, sir?

Orsino

I cannot be so answered.

Viola

                    Sooth, but you must.

1   *their love may be called appetite, / No*
     motion of the liver, but the palate

     **I.e., their love is not an intense
     appetite of the *liver* (believed to be
     the seat of passion) but a minor
     appetite, like the craving of the
     palate for food.**

2   *That suffer surfeit, cloyment, and revolt*

     **That indulges to the point of
     excess, satiety, and (eventually)
     revulsion**

3   *like a worm i' the bud*

     **Like a cankerworm hidden in a
     flower (and feeding upon it)**

4   *damask*

     Mingled pink and white; rosy

5   *green and yellow*

     **Pale, nauseated (the pallor of the
     melancholy person)**

Say that some lady, as perhaps there is,
Hath for your love as great a pang of heart
As you have for Olivia. You cannot love her;   90
You tell her so. Must she not then be answered?

Orsino

There is no woman's sides

endure   Can bide° the beating of so strong a passion
As love doth give my heart; no woman's heart

consistency   So big to hold so much. They lack retention.°   95
Alas, their love may be called appetite,

i.e., emotion No motion° of the liver, but the palate, [1]
That suffer surfeit, cloyment, and revolt; [2]
But mine is all as hungry as the sea

comparison   And can digest as much. Make no compare°   100
Between that love a woman can bear me

feel for   And that I owe° Olivia.

Viola

                        Ay, but I know—

Orsino

What dost thou know?

Viola

Too well what love women to men may owe.
In faith, they are as true of heart as we.   105
My father had a daughter loved a man
As it might be, perhaps, were I a woman,
I should your lordship.

Orsino

                        And what's her history?

Viola

A blank, my lord. She never told her love,
But let concealment, like a worm i' th' bud, [3]   110
Feed on her damask [4] cheek. She pined in thought,
And with a green and yellow [5] melancholy

1   *like patience on a monument, / Smiling at grief*

Like a statue on a tomb representing patience, wearing a smile despite its grief. (The image is, however, possibly of two personified figures, Patience and Grief, in spite of the fact that the Folio only capitalizes *Patience*.)

2   *Our shows are more than will*

Our professions of love are greater than our desire.

3   *give no place, bide no denay*

Yield to nobody, accept no rejection

She sat like patience on a monument,

Smiling at grief. [1] Was not this love indeed?

We men may say more, swear more, but indeed 115

always Our shows are more than will, [2] for still° we prove

Much in our vows but little in our love.

Orsino

But died thy sister of her love, my boy?

Viola

I am all the daughters of my father's house,

And all the brothers too—and yet I know not. 120

go to Sir, shall I to° this lady?

Orsino

                      Ay, that's the theme:

To her in haste. Give her this jewel. Say

My love can give no place, bide no denay. [3]

                              [He hands her a jewel.]

                             They exit [in different directions].

1 *Come thy ways*

   Come along

2 *let me be boiled to death with melancholy*

   I.e., let me be sad forever. *Boiled* is a pun on "biled," that is, filled with bile, the bodily fluid that, in excess, was thought to cause melancholy.

3 *sheep-biter*

   A seemingly aggressive dog that attacks sheep from behind; hence, a sneaky, mean-spirited person.

4 *bear-baiting*

   A form of popular entertainment in Shakespeare's day, in which dogs attacked chained bears; see 1.3.85 and note. Puritans opposed this form of public entertainment (and others), and outlawed it in 1642 when they came to power in England.

5 *my metal of India*

   My golden one; my treasure (with a pun on "mettle"). India probably refers here to the West Indies, which Europeans believed had abundant gold ready to be mined.

6 *practicing behavior to his own shadow*

   I.e., striking courtly poses by himself

Act 2, Scene 5

Enter **Sir Toby** [**Belch**], **Sir Andrew**, *and* **Fabian**.

Sir Toby Belch

Come thy ways, [1] Signior Fabian.

Fabian

little bit   Nay, I'll come. If I lose a scruple° of this sport, let me be
boiled to death with melancholy. [2]

Sir Toby Belch

petty   Wouldst thou not be glad to have the niggardly,° ras-
cally sheep-biter [3] come by some notable shame?   5

Fabian

celebrate   I would exult,° man. You know he brought me out o'
favor with my lady about a bear-baiting [4] here.

Sir Toby Belch

To anger him, we'll have the bear again, and we will
mock   fool° him black and blue. Shall we not, Sir Andrew?

Sir Andrew

If   An° we do not, it is pity of our lives.   10

Enter **Maria**.

Sir Toby Belch

Here comes the little villain.——How now, my metal of
India? [5]

Maria

(an evergreen hedge)   Get you all three into the boxtree.° Malvolio's coming
down this walk. He has been yonder i' the sun practic-
ing behavior to his own shadow [6] this half hour.   15
Observe him, for the love of mockery, for I know this
Hide   letter will make a contemplative idiot of him. Close,° in
the name of jesting!   [*They hide.*]

1   *trout that must be caught with tickling*

    I.e., person who'll be tricked and
    captured by flattery. Trout in
    shallow water can sometimes be
    caught by stroking their gills as
    they swim.

2   *'Tis but fortune*

    It's nothing but (fickle) fortune.

3   *come thus near*

    Say similar things

4   *turkey-cock*

    Male turkey (which struts and
    preens); a proverbial image of self-
    importance.

5   *How he jets under his advanced plumes!*

    How he struts about with his
    feathers on display!

6   *'Slight*

    By God's light (i.e., "For God's sake")

7   *the yeoman of the wardrobe*

    The servant in charge of clothing
    and linen. Scholars are uncertain
    whether the *Lady of the Strachy* and
    her *yeoman of the wardrobe* refer to a
    specific example of a socially
    unequal marriage that would have
    been known to Shakespeare's
    audience.

Lie thou there [*drops a letter*], for here comes the trout
that must be caught with tickling. [1]   [*She exits.*] 20

Enter Malvolio.

Malvolio

'Tis but fortune; [2] all is fortune. Maria once told me
i.e., Olivia / care for   she° did affect° me, and I have heard herself come thus
fall in love   near, [3] that, should she fancy,° it should be one of my
temperament / treats   complexion.° Besides, she uses° me with a more
exalted respect than anyone else that follows her. What 25
should I think on 't?

Sir Toby Belch

arrogant   [*aside*] Here's an overweening° rogue!

Fabian

[*aside*] Oh, peace! Contemplation makes a rare turkey-
cock [4] of him. How he jets under his advanced plumes! [5]

Sir Andrew

[*aside*] 'Slight, [6] I could so beat the rogue!   30

Sir Toby Belch

[*to* **Sir Andrew**] Peace, I say.

Malvolio

To be Count Malvolio!

Sir Toby Belch

[*aside*] Ah, rogue!

Sir Andrew

Shoot   [*aside*] Pistol° him; pistol him.

Sir Toby Belch

[*to* **Sir Andrew**] Peace, peace!   35

Malvolio

precedent   There is example° for 't. The Lady of the Strachy
married the yeoman of the wardrobe. [7]

1   *Jezebel*
    **In the Bible (2 Kings 9), King Ahab's
    arrogant widow**

2   *deeply in*
    **Caught up deeply in his own
    fantasies**

3   *blows him*
    Puffs him up

4   *my state*
    **My chair of state. Malvolio
    imagines himself as a nobleman,
    which he would become were he to
    marry Olivia, a countess.**

5   *stone-bow*
    **Catapult or sling that shoots small
    stones**

6   *branched*
    **Decorated with (embroidered)
    leaves and branches**

7   *to have the humor of state*
    **To affect the lofty manner fit for
    my position**

8   *after a demure travel of regard*
    **After solemnly surverying the
    room**

9   *Bolts and shackles!*
    **(Put him in) handcuffs and ankle
    irons! Toby is incensed by
    Malvolio's presumption.**

10 *make out for him*
    Go to summon him

Sir Andrew

[*aside*] Fie on him, Jezebel! [1]

Fabian

[*to* **Sir Andrew**] Oh, peace! Now he's deeply in. [2] Look
how imagination blows him. [3]   40

Malvolio

Having been three months married to her, sitting in
my state [4]—

Sir Toby Belch

[*aside*] Oh, for a stone-bow, [5] to hit him in the eye!

Malvolio

household servants   Calling my officers° about me, in my branched [6] velvet
gown, having come from a daybed, where I have left   45
Olivia sleeping—

Sir Toby Belch

[*aside*] Fire and brimstone!

Fabian

[*to* **Sir Toby Belch**] Oh, peace, peace!

Malvolio

And then to have the humor of state, [7] and, after a
demure travel of regard, [8] telling them I know my place   50
as I would they should do theirs, to ask for my kinsman
Toby—

Sir Toby Belch

[*aside*] Bolts and shackles! [9]

Fabian

[*to* **Sir Toby Belch**] Oh peace, peace, peace! Now, now.

Malvolio

Seven of my people, with an obedient start, make out   55
perhaps   for him. [10] I frown the while, and perchance° wind up
my watch, or play with my—some rich jewel. Toby
bows   approaches, curtsies° there to me—

1   *drawn from us with cars*

Forced out of us by torture.
Prisoners under interrogation
were sometimes tied between two
cars, or horse-drawn carts, that
were then driven in opposite
directions.

2   *an austere regard of control*

A stern look of authority.

3   *take you a blow o' the lips*

Give you a punch in the mouth.

4   *break the sinews of our plot*

I.e., ruin our plan

Sir Toby Belch

[*aside*] Shall this fellow live?

Fabian

[*to* **Sir Toby Belch**] Though our silence be drawn from   60
us with cars,¹ yet peace.

Malvolio

friendly I extend my hand to him thus, quenching my familiar°
smile with an austere regard of control²—

Sir Toby Belch

[*aside*] And does not Toby take you a blow o' the lips³
then?   65

Malvolio

Saying, "Cousin Toby, my fortunes, having cast me on
your niece, give me this prerogative of speech—"

Sir Toby Belch

[*aside*] What, what?

Malvolio

"You must amend your drunkenness."

Sir Toby Belch

[*aside*] Out, scab!   70

Fabian

[*to* **Sir Toby Belch**] Nay, patience, or we break the sinews
of our plot.⁴

Malvolio

"Besides, you waste the treasure of your time with a
foolish knight—"

Sir Andrew

[*aside*] That's me, I warrant you.   75

Malvolio

"One Sir Andrew—"

Sir Andrew

[*aside*] I knew 'twas I, for many do call me fool.

Malvolio

business [*seeing the letter*] What employment° have we here?

1   *Now is the woodcock near the gin.*

    Now the bird is near the engine (i.e., the trap). Woodcocks were known as particularly stupid birds, and easy to catch.

2   *And the spirit of humors intimate reading aloud to him!*

    I.e., and may his mood suggest to him that he read out loud.

3   *her very c's, her u's, and her t's*

    The letters spell out *cut*, a slang word for female genitalia.

4   *her great P's*

    I.e., her uppercase letter P. The pun on *pee* (in Shakespeare's day, as now, a synonym for "urine") continues the bawdy wordplay in the previous line.

5   *in contempt of question*

    Beyond question

6   *By your leave, wax.*

    Malvolio asks the sealing wax for permission to open the letter.

7   *And the impressure her Lucrece, with which she uses to seal.*

    Olivia's signet ring (used to seal the wax on a letter) is embossed with the image of Lucrece, a Roman matron famous for having committed suicide in the wake of a rape brought on by her husband's boast of her chastity. In Shakespeare's narrative poem *The Rape of Lucrece* (1594), the heroine kills herself in order to prevent any future unchaste women from using her reputation as a cover story for licentious behavior, hence the image of the Lucrece knife at line 101 that serves as a symbol of the chaste silencing of female desire. Malvolio's breaking of the seal on the letter is thus itself a kind of violation, one that perhaps rehearses in a physical key his earlier alphabetical speculation on her genitalia. *Soft!* at line 88 could either mean "Wait a minute," or it could be a reference to the yet malleable state of the sealing wax, easy to breach.

8   *The numbers altered.*

    The meter (of the verse) is changed.

9   *brock*

    Badger (perhaps because badgers are black and white, the colors in which the "puritan" Malvolio could be dressed)

10 *a Lucrece knife*

    The knife with which Lucrece stabbed herself (see line 89–90).

Fabian

[*aside*] Now is the woodcock near the gin. ¹

Sir Toby Belch

[*to* **Fabian**] Oh, peace! And the spirit of humors   80
intimate reading aloud to him! ²

Malvolio

handwriting [*picking up the letter*] By my life, this is my lady's hand.°
These be her very c's, her u's, and her t's, ³ and thus
makes she her great P's. ⁴ It is, in contempt of question, ⁵
her hand.   85

Sir Andrew

[*aside*] Her c's, her u's, and her t's? Why that?

Malvolio

[*reads*] "To the unknown beloved, this, and my good
wishes"—Her very phrases! By your leave, wax. ⁶ Soft!
And the impressure her Lucrece, with which she uses to
seal. ⁷ 'Tis my lady. To whom should this be? [*He opens   90
the letter.*]

Fabian

[*aside*] This wins him, liver and all.

Malvolio

[*reads*] "Jove knows I love,
But who?
Lips, do not move;
No man must know."   95

"No man must know." What follows? The numbers
altered. ⁸ "No man must know." If this should be thee,
Malvolio!

Sir Toby Belch

[*aside*] Marry, hang thee, brock! ⁹

Malvolio

[*reads*] "I may command where I adore,   100
But silence, like a Lucrece knife, ¹⁰

1 *M.O.A.I.*

The letters of course are in
Malvolio's name but don't appear
in this order. Scholars have not
been any quicker than Malvolio to
solve this riddle, though see 2.3.9
and LONGER NOTE, page 288;
another suggestion is that it is an
anagram of "I am O" (i.e., Olivia),
but that Malvolio narcissisticly
applies it to himself

2 *And with what wing the staniel checks at it!*

And how excitedly the hawk spots
its prey!

3 *formal capacity*

Functioning intellect

4 *make up that*

Make something out of that

5 *He is now at a cold scent.*

He's now like a hunting dog that
has lost the scent of the fox it trails.

6 *Sowter will cry upon 't for all this,*
though it be as rank as a fox.

This *Sowter* (apparently a dog's
name) will bark loudly when he
picks up the scent. *Though it be rank*
as a fox may mean either (1) as if that
smell were as strong as a fox's; (2)
even though a fox has crossed the
trail with its strong scent (which
might distract the dog).

7 *excellent at faults*

Excellent at picking up scents that
have gone cold

8 *there is no consonancy in the sequel*

There's no logic in the ordering of
the subsequent letters

stab   With bloodless stroke my heart doth gore.°

      M.O.A.I. [1] doth sway my life."

Fabian

pretentious   [*aside*] A fustian° riddle!

Sir Toby Belch

[*aside*] Excellent wench, say I.   105

Malvolio

"M.O.A.I. doth sway my life." Nay, but first, let me see, let me see, let me see.

Fabian

prepared for   [*aside*] What dish o' poison has she dressed° him!

Sir Toby Belch

[*aside*] And with what wing the staniel checks at it! [2]

Malvolio

"I may command where I adore." Why, she may com-   110
mand me. I serve her; she is my lady. Why, this is evident
hindrance   to any formal capacity. [3] There is no obstruction° in this.
arrangement   And the end: what should that alphabetical position°
portend? If I could make that resemble something in
me. Softly! "M.O.A.I."—   115

Sir Toby Belch

[*aside*] Oh, ay, make up that. [4]—He is now at a cold scent. [5]

Fabian

[*aside*] Sowter will cry upon 't for all this, though it be as
rank as a fox. [6]

Malvolio

"M"—Malvolio. "M"! Why, that begins my name.

Fabian

[*aside*] Did not I say he would work it out? The cur is   120
excellent at faults. [7]

Malvolio

"M." But then there is no consonancy in the sequel. [8]

1   *And "O" shall end*

Either (1) the letter *O*, the final
letter in Malvolio's name, will
come last; (2) Malvolio will shout
out in pain at the end of the
scheme; or (3) a noose, which has
the shape of the letter *O*, will be
Malvolio's fate.

2   *This simulation is not as the former*

This riddle is not like the earlier
one (referring to *I may command
where I adore*, line 100, which
Malvolio took as a clear reference
to himself).

3   *open their hands*

I.e., are bounteous with their gifts

4   *humble slough*

Give up your humble behavior (as a
snake casts off its *slough*, or dead
skin).

5   *arguments of state*

Political topics

6   *Put thyself into the trick of singularity.*

In this way, make yourself unique.

7   *yellow stockings . . . cross-gartered*

Yellow was considered the color of
love in general and jealousy in
particular; the fact that Malvolio
has been known to wear yellow
stockings prior to this
recommendation suggests some
previous attempt at romantic self-
stylization on his part. One
contemporary song from the
period, a nostalgic plaint for a

bachelorhood lost to the confines
of marriage, contains the refrain
"Give me my yellow hose again,
give me my yellow hose" (see Ross
Duffin's *Shakespeare's Songbook*,
314). Garters were used to hold up
stockings, and it is thought that
the extra flourish of cross- (as
opposed to regular) gartering
indicated a lover living in hope, as
opposed to someone whose
garters were not tied, and whose
slipping stockings indicated a
dishevelment beyond care.

8   *Go to*

An expression usually either of
impatience or, as here, of
anticipation; like "let's go," or
"come on."

9   *alter services*

Trade positions (and therefore
become the servant to your master)

10 *She that would alter services with thee, /
The Fortunate Unhappy.*

These two phrases function as the
complimentary close and
signature of the letter.

closer examination That suffers under probation°: "A" should follow, but
"O" does.

Fabian

[*aside*] And "O" shall end,[1] I hope.   125

Sir Toby Belch

[*aside*] Ay, or I'll cudgel him and make him cry "Oh!"

Malvolio

And then "I" comes behind.

Fabian

if [*aside*] Ay, an° you had any eye behind you, you might see
ridicule more detraction° at your heels than fortunes before
you.   130

letter to Malvolio from Maria in Olivia's

Malvolio

"M.O.A.I." This simulation is not as the former,[2] and yet,
force / yield to crush° this a little, it would bow° to me, for every one of
these letters are in my name. Soft; here follows prose.
consider / fortunes [*reads*] "If this fall into thy hand, revolve.° In my stars° I
am above thee, but be not afraid of greatness. Some   135
are born great, some achieve greatness, and some have
greatness thrust upon 'em. Thy fates open their hands.[3]
accustom Let thy blood and spirit embrace them, and, to inure°
likely thyself to what thou art like° to be, cast thy humble
antagonistic slough[4] and appear fresh. Be opposite° with a kinsman,   140
ring out with surly with servants. Let thy tongue tang° arguments of
state.[5] Put thyself into the trick of singularity.[6] She
thus advises thee that sighs for thee. Remember who
commended thy yellow stockings and wished to see
thee ever cross-gartered.[7] I say remember. Go to,[8] thou 145
art made, if thou desir'st to be so; if not, let me see thee
a steward still, the fellow of servants, and not worthy
to touch Fortune's fingers. Farewell.
She that would alter services[9] with thee,
The Fortunate Unhappy."[10]   150

1   *politic*

    Political (see lines 141–142)

2   *baffle*

    **I.e., humiliate. To *baffle* a knight
    was to strip him of his knighthood.**

3   *wash off gross acquaintance*

    **Stop associating with vulgar,
    common folk**

4   *I will be point-devise the very man*

    **I will in every detail become the
    man described in this letter**

5   *drives me to these habits of her liking*

    Makes me wear the clothes she likes

6   *even with the swiftness of putting on*

    I.e., as fast as I can put them on

7   *Sophy*

    Shah of Persia

open countryside / reveals   Daylight and champaign° discovers° not more. This is

obvious   open.° I will be proud; I will read politic[1] authors; I will

baffle[2] Sir Toby; I will wash off gross acquaintance;[3] I

will be point-devise the very man.[4] I do not now fool

trick   myself, to let imagination jade° me, for every reason   155

excites to this: that my lady loves me. She did com-

mend my yellow stockings of late, she did praise my leg

being cross-gartered, and in this she manifests herself

to my love, and, with a kind of injunction, drives me to

fortunate   these habits of her liking.[5] I thank my stars; I am happy!°   160

aloof / proud   I will be strange,° stout,° in yellow stockings, and cross-

gartered, even with the swiftness of putting on.[6] Jove

and my stars be praised! Here is yet a postscript.

[*reads*] "Thou canst not choose but know who I am. If

accept   thou entertain'st° my love, let it appear in thy smiling.   165

Thy smiles become thee well. Therefore in my presence

always   still° smile, dear my sweet, I prithee."

Jove, I thank thee! I will smile. I will do everything that

thou wilt have me.   *He exits.*

Fabian

I will not give my part of this sport for a pension of   170

thousands to be paid from the Sophy.[7]

Sir Toby Belch

plot   I could marry this wench for this device.°

Sir Andrew

So could I too.

Sir Toby Belch

And ask no other dowry with her but such another jest.

Sir Andrew

Nor I neither.   175

Enter **Maria.**

1   *Wilt thou set thy foot o' my neck?*

    I.e., shall I bow down before you?

2   *Shall I play my freedom at tray-trip and become thy bondslave?*

    Shall I bet my liberty in a dice game (in which the goal is to throw a three) and (when I lose) become your slave?

3   *notable contempt*

    Prominent object of scorn

4   *To the gates of Tartar*

    The gates of hell; *Tartarus* is the lowest part of the underworld in Greek mythology.

Fabian

con artist Here comes my noble gull-catcher.°

Sir Toby Belch

[*to* **Maria**] Wilt thou set thy foot o' my neck?[1]

Sir Andrew

[*to* **Maria**] Or o' mine either?

Sir Toby Belch

[*to* **Maria**] Shall I play my freedom at tray-trip and
become thy bondslave?[2]   *180*

Sir Andrew

[*to* **Maria**] I' faith, or I either?

Sir Toby Belch

[*to* **Maria**] Why, thou hast put him in such a dream that
when the image of it leaves him he must run mad.

Maria

Nay, but say true: does it work upon him?

Sir Toby Belch

strong liquor Like aqua-vitae° with a midwife.   *185*

Maria

If you will then see the fruits of the sport, mark his first
approach before my lady. He will come to her in yellow
stockings, and 'tis a color she abhors, and cross-gartered,
a fashion she detests. And he will smile upon her, which
will now be so unsuitable to her disposition, being   *190*
addicted to a melancholy as she is, that it cannot but turn
him into a notable contempt.[3] If you will see it, follow
me.

Sir Toby Belch

To the gates of Tartar,[4] thou most excellent devil of wit!

Sir Andrew

join in I'll make one° too.   *They exit.* *195*

1   tabor

    A small drum

2   *Dost thou live by*

    **Do you make your living playing
    (though Feste takes *live by* to mean
    "live near")**

3   *lies by*

    Lives near, but also "sleeps next to"

4   *stands by*

    **Is near, but also "is supported
    financially by"**

5   *this age*

    This period in which we now live

6   *They that dally nicely with words may
    quickly make them wanton.*

    **Those who make clever plays on
    words soon render their meanings
    unstable. Feste's following lines
    pun on alternate meanings of *dally*
    (play sexually) and *wanton*
    (promiscuous, unchaste).**

7   *since bonds disgraced them*

    **I.e., since legal agreements
    replaced a person's spoken words
    as guarantors of trustworthiness**

Act 3, Scene 1

Enter [from separate doors] **Viola** *and* Clown, [**Feste**, *carrying a tabor*[1]].

Viola

God save | Save° thee, friend, and thy music. Dost thou live by[2] thy tabor?

Feste

No, sir, I live by the church.

Viola

clergyman | Art thou a churchman?°

Feste

No such matter, sir. I do live by the church, for I do live   5
at my house, and my house doth stand by the church.

Viola

So thou mayst say the king lies by[3] a beggar if a beggar
dwell near him, or the church stands by[4] thy tabor, if
thy tabor stand by the church.

Feste

It's as you / maxim | You° have said, sir. To see this age![5] A sentence° is but a   10
soft goat skin | cheveril° glove to a good wit. How quickly the wrong
side may be turned outward!

Viola

Nay, that's certain. They that dally nicely with words
may quickly make them wanton.[6]

Feste

I would therefore my sister had had no name, sir.   15

Viola

Why, man?

Feste

Why, sir, her name's a word, and to dally with that
word might make my sister wanton. But, indeed,
words are very rascals since bonds disgraced them.[7]

1   *pilchards*

A type of fish, related to herrings
but smaller.

2   *the fool should be as oft with your*
    master as with my mistress

(1) I should be able to bring my
fooling to Orsino as well as Olivia;
(2) Orsino deserves to be called *fool*
just as much as Olivia.

3   *I think I saw your wisdom there*

Feste suggests that Cesario
shouldn't chide him for being at
Orsino's house, since he has
recently seen Cesario at Olivia's
house (who is similarly not
Cesario's proper master). Feste
pokes fun at Cesario by calling him
your wisdom, a mockingly formal
title, in response to Cesario
identifying him as Olivia's fool
(line 28).

4   *pass upon*

Thrust at (a fencing term), though
here referring to Feste's wit; possibly
also "pass judgment upon."

Viola

Thy reason, man?   20

Feste

In truth Troth,° sir, I can yield you none without words, and
words are grown so false I am loath to prove reason
with them.

Viola

guarantee I warrant° thou art a merry fellow and car'st for nothing.

Feste

Not so, sir; I do care for something. But in my con-   25
science, sir, I do not care for you. If that be to care for
nothing, sir, I would it would make you invisible.

Viola

Art not thou the Lady Olivia's fool?

Feste

No, indeed, sir. The Lady Olivia has no folly. She will
keep no fool, sir, till she be married, and fools are as   30
like husbands as pilchards¹ are to herrings: the
husband's the bigger. I am indeed not her fool, but her
corrupter of words.

Viola

recently I saw thee late° at the Count Orsino's.

Feste

i.e., Earth Foolery, sir, does walk about the orb° like the sun: it   35
if it were not that shines everywhere. I would be sorry, sir, but° the fool
should be as oft with your master as with my mistress;²
I think I saw your wisdom there.³

Viola

if Nay, an° thou pass upon⁴ me, I'll no more with thee.
Hold, there's expenses for thee. [*gives another coin*]   40

Feste

shipment Now Jove, in his next commodity° of hair, send thee a
beard!

1   *almost sick for one*

     **Desperate to grow a beard; but
     also "sick with love for a man"**

2   *Would not a pair of these have bred, sir?*

     **Wouldn't two such coins (as Viola
     has given Feste) have produced
     offspring? Feste is attempting to
     get more money out of Viola.**

3   *put to use*

     **(1) i.e., allowed to mate;
     (2) invested**

4   *Lord Pandarus of Phrygia, sir, to bring a
     Cressida to this Troilus*

     **The fictional Greek lovers Troilus
     and Cressida were brought
     together by Cressida's uncle,
     Pandarus.**

5   *begging but a beggar. Cressida was a
     beggar.*

     **Feste's meaning is that in asking
     for a *Cressida* to pair with *Troilus* (i.e.,
     asking for a second coin) he is not
     asking for much, since Cressida (or
     at least in Robert Henryson's late
     15th-century version of the story)
     became a leprous beggar in her old
     age.**

6   *out of my welkin*

     I.e., none of my concern

7   *I might say "element"*

     ***Welkin* and *element* are both
     pedantic synonyms for "sky" or
     "air."**

8   *And, like the haggard, check at every
     feather / That comes before his eye*

     **And, like a wild hawk, strike at
     every potential prey that it sees**

9   *folly that he wisely shows is fit, / But wise
     men, folly-fall'n, quite taint their wit*

     **Folly deliberately enacted is
     appropriate (for Feste, a
     professional fool), but a wise man
     who falls into folly discredits his
     intelligence.**

Viola

faith   By my troth,° I'll tell thee, I am almost sick for one, ¹

[*aside*] though I would not have it grow on my chin.

[*to* **Feste**] Is thy lady within?   45

Feste

Would not a pair of these have bred, sir? ²

Viola

Yes, being kept together and put to use. ³

Feste

I would play Lord Pandarus of Phrygia, sir, to bring a

Cressida to this Troilus. ⁴

Viola

I understand you, sir. 'Tis well begged. [*gives another coin*]   50

Feste

The matter, I hope, is not great, sir, begging but a beg-

gar. Cressida was a beggar. ⁵ My lady is within, sir. I will

explain   conster° to them whence you come. Who you are and

what you would are out of my welkin; ⁶ I might say

overused   "element," ⁷ but the word is overworn.°   *He exits.* 55

Viola

This fellow is wise enough to play the fool,

requires   And to do that well craves° a kind of wit.

He must observe their mood on whom he jests,

nature   The quality° of persons and the time,

And, like the haggard, check at every feather   60

talent   That comes before his eye. ⁸ This is a practice°

As full of labor as a wise man's art,

For folly that he wisely shows is fit,

But wise men, folly-fall'n, quite taint their wit. ⁹

Enter **Sir Toby** [**Belch**]*and* [**Sir**] **Andrew**.

1   Dieu vous garde, monsieur.

    God save you, sir. (French)

2   Et vous aussi. Votre serviteur!

    **And you as well. (I am) your
    servant! (French)**

3   *encounter*

    **Enter. Sir Toby speaks with mock
    courtliness, in response to what he
    sees as Sir Andrew and Viola's
    pretentious exchange.**

4   *gait and entrance*

    **Walking and entering (with a
    possible play on "gate," as *gait* is
    spelled in the 1623 Folio)**

5   *the heavens rain odors on you*

    **May Heaven drop perfume on you
    (i.e., bless you).**

Sir Toby Belch

i.e., God save   Save° you, gentleman.   65

Viola

And you, sir.

Sir Andrew

Dieu vous garde, monsieur. [1]

Viola

Et vous aussi. Votre serviteur! [2]

Sir Andrew

I hope, sir, you are, and I am yours.

Sir Toby Belch

Will you encounter [3] the house? My niece is desirous   70

purpose   you should enter, if your trade° be to her.

Viola

toward / destination   I am bound to° your niece, sir. I mean, she is the list° of

my voyage.

Sir Toby Belch

Try   Taste° your legs, sir. Put them to motion.

Viola

stand up under   My legs do better understand° me, sir, than I under-   75

stand what you mean by bidding me taste my legs.

Sir Toby Belch

I mean to go, sir, to enter.

Viola

I will answer you with gait and entrance [4] —but we are

anticipated   prevented.°

Enter **Olivia** *and [* **Maria**, *her] gentlewoman.*

Most excellent accomplished lady, the heavens rain   80

odors on you! [5]

Sir Andrew

excellent / Well said   [*aside*] That youth's a rare° courtier. "Rain odors." Well!°

1 *My matter hath no voice*

My message must not be spoken aloud.

2 *vouchsafed*

Willingly offered; attentive

3 *I'll get 'em all three all ready.*

I'll learn all these three words by heart (to use myself).

4 *'Twas never merry world / Since lowly feigning was called compliment.*

The world has not been the same since false humility (such as Cesario displays when he calls Olivia his mistress) came to be considered genuinely courteous. *'Twas never a merry world* was a proverbial formulation to introduce a sense of the decline of the present age.

5 *blanks*

Empty sheets of paper

6 *But would you undertake another suit*

But if you would ask for something else

Viola

except

receptive

My matter hath no voice, [1] lady, but° to your own most
pregnant° and vouchsafed [2] ear.

Sir Andrew

[*aside*] "Odors," "pregnant," and "vouchsafed." I'll get 85
'em all three all ready. [3]

Olivia

Let the garden door be shut and leave me to my hearing.

[**Sir Toby Belch**, **Sir Andrew**, *and* **Maria** *exit.*]

Give me your hand, sir.

Viola

My duty, madam, and most humble service.

Olivia

What is your name? 90

Viola

Cesario is your servant's name, fair princess.

Olivia

My servant, sir? 'Twas never merry world
Since lowly feigning was called compliment. [4]
You're servant to the Count Orsino, youth.

Viola

what is his

And he is yours, and his° must needs be yours: 95
Your servant's servant is your servant, madam.

Olivia

As for

For° him, I think not on him. For his thoughts,
Would they were blanks [5] rather than filled with me.

Viola

Madam, I come to whet your gentle thoughts
On his behalf.

Olivia

Oh, by your leave, I pray you; 100
I bade you never speak again of him—
But would you undertake another suit, [6]

1　*music from the spheres*

The 1st-century Egyptian astrologer Ptolemy theorized that other planets orbited the Earth in crystalline spheres, in the process making sublimely beautiful sounds that only the gods could hear.

2　*I fear me*

I am afraid.

3　*Have you not set mine honor at the stake / And baited it with all th' unmuzzled thoughts / That tyrannous heart can think?*

The image in this passage is taken from bear-baiting (see 1.3.85 and note). Olivia believes that she is being harshly judged for her unbecoming conduct, and so imagines her honor as a bear being attacked by Cesario's ferocious thoughts.

4　*Enough is shown*

No more needs to be said

5　*A cypress, not a bosom, / Hides my heart.*

A thin, gaudy fabric, not flesh, conceals my heart (thereby rendering it visible). *Cypress* here refers not to the tree but to "Cyprus" linen.

6　*vulgar proof*

Common experience

argue for   I had rather hear you to solicit° that
Than music from the spheres.[1]

Viola

                     Dear lady—

Olivia

opportunity to speak   Give me leave,° beseech you. I did send,   *admits*   105
After the last enchantment you did here,   *giving Malvolio*
wrong   A ring in chase of you. So did I abuse°   *a ring.*
Myself, my servant, and, I fear me,[2] you.
assessment   Under your hard construction° must I sit,
trick   To force that on you in a shameful cunning°   110
was not anything   Which you knew none° of yours. What might you
       think?
Have you not set mine honor at the stake
And baited it with all th' unmuzzled thoughts
perceptiveness   That tyrannous heart can think?[3] To one of your receiving°
Enough is shown.[4] A cypress, not a bosom,   115
Hides my heart.[5] So, let me hear you speak.

Viola

I pity you.

Olivia

step   That's a degree° to love.

Viola

step   No, not a grece,° for 'tis a vulgar proof[6]
That very oft we pity enemies.

Olivia

Why then methinks 'tis time to smile again.   120
ready   O world, how apt° the poor are to be proud!
If one should be a prey, how much the better
To fall before the lion than the wolf!   (*Clock strikes.*)
chides / for   The clock upbraids° me with° the waste of time.

1 *westward ho*

Ferrymen on the River Thames in
London cried "Westward Ho!"
when embarking from the City of
London to the royal palace at
Westminster.

2 *you do think you are not what you are*

Viola accuses Olivia of not
understanding the reality of her
situation. Most obviously, this
refers to the fact that Olivia
believes herself to be in love with a
man; it may also refer to Olivia's
inappropriate affection for a
supposed subordinate, or to the
sudden abandonment of her vow
to remain chaste until the
completion of her mourning
period.

3 *I think the same of you*

Probably "I think you are better
than a mere servant."

4 *Love's night is noon.*

Love is as obvious as the noon sun
(i.e., it can't be hidden).

5 *Do not extort thy reasons from this
clause, / For that I woo, thou therefore
hast no cause*

Do not decide that because I have
just declared my love for you, you
now have no cause (to declare your
own love).

Be not afraid, good youth; I will not have you. 125

And yet when wit and youth is come to harvest,

handsome   Your wife is like to reap a proper° man.

There lies your way, due west.

Viola

                   Then westward ho! [1]

composure   Grace and good disposition° attend your Ladyship!

send nothing   You'll nothing,° madam, to my lord by me? 130

Olivia

Stay, I prithee; tell me what thou think'st of me.

Viola

That you do think you are not what you are. [2]

Olivia

If I think so, I think the same of you. [3]

Viola

Then think you right: I am not what I am.

Olivia

I would you were as I would have you be. 135

Viola

Would it be better, madam, than I am?

i.e., might be better   I wish it might,° for now I am your fool.

Olivia

[*aside*] Oh, what a deal of scorn looks beautiful

In the contempt and anger of his lip.

A murd'rous guilt shows not itself more soon 140

Than love that would seem hid. Love's night is noon. [4]

[*to* **Viola**] Cesario, by the roses of the spring,

By maidhood, honor, truth, and everything,

in spite of   I love thee so, that, maugre° all thy pride,

Neither   Nor° wit nor reason can my passion hide. 145

statement   Do not extort thy reasons from this clause,°

For that I woo, thou therefore hast no cause, [5]

1   *But rather reason thus with reason fetter*

    **But instead, counter that thought
    with this idea**

2   *never none*

    Not anyone ever

3   *my master's tears to you deplore*

    **Complain to you of Orsino's
    suffering**

But rather reason thus with reason fetter:[1]
Love sought is good, but given unsought is better.
Viola
By innocence I swear, and by my youth,   150
I have one heart, one bosom, and one truth,
And that no woman has, nor never none[2]
Shall mistress be of it, save I alone.
And so adieu, good madam. Nevermore
Will I my master's tears to you deplore.[3]   155
Olivia
Yet come again, for thou perhaps mayst move
That heart, which now abhors, to like his love.

They exit [in different directions].

- Olivia declared love for Viola & Viola
says you don't know who I am

- Olivia asks her to come back at the
end if her mind changed

- Last 16 lines is rhymed couplets

1   *venom*

    Venomous (angry) person

2   *they*

    I.e., *judgment* and *reason*

3   *since before Noah was a sailor*

    **I.e., for a very long time. The
    biblical story of Noah and his ark is
    told in Genesis: 6–9.**

4   *fire-new from the mint*

    I.e., newly coined; brand new

Act 3, Scene 2

Enter **Sir Toby [Belch]**, **Sir Andrew**, *and* **Fabian**.

Sir Andrew

moment   No, faith, I'll not stay a jot° longer.

Sir Toby Belch

The reason, dear venom?[1] Give thy reason.

Fabian

reveal   You must needs yield° your reason, Sir Andrew.

Sir Andrew

Marry, I saw your niece do more favors to the Count's

servingman than ever she bestowed upon me. I saw 't   5

garden   i'th' orchard.°

Sir Toby Belch

Did she see thee the while, old boy? Tell me that.

Sir Andrew

As plain as I see you now.

Fabian

proof   This was a great argument° of love in her toward you.

Sir Andrew

By God's light   'Slight,° will you make an ass o' me?   10

Fabian

to be valid   I will prove it legitimate,° sir, upon the oaths of judg-

ment and reason.

Sir Toby Belch

jurors   And they[2] have been grand-jurymen° since before

Noah was a sailor.[3]

Fabian

She did show favor to the youth in your sight only to   15

i.e., sleeping   exasperate you, to awake your dormouse° valor, to put

fire in your heart and brimstone in your liver. You

should then have accosted her, and with some excel-

lent jests, fire-new from the mint,[4] you should have

1   *at your hand*
I.e., from you

2   *double gilt of this opportunity*
This twice-golden opportunity

3   *you are now sailed into the north of my lady's opinion*
I.e., now Olivia's affections for you have cooled

4   *a Dutchman's beard*
This may be a topical reference to William Barentz, a Dutchman who led a famous expedition to the Arctic in 1596.

5   *Brownist*
A follower of the radical Protestant extremist preacher Robert Browne

6   *build me*
I.e., build. The *me*, like that following *challenge* in the following line, is merely an intensifier, sometimes called (following Latin usage) the ethical dative.

7   *license of ink*
I.e., freedom to say things on paper (that you would not dare to say to someone's face)

8   *"thou"-est*
I.e., use the "thou" form of the second-person pronoun when you address him (which to a stranger was insulting, as it was often used for social inferiors).

9   *bed of Ware*
A well-known bed, nearly eleven feet square. It was originally housed in various inns throughout the town of Ware, becoming a tourist attraction due to its great size. The bed is currently on display at the Victoria & Albert Museum, London.

10   *gall*
(1) bitterness; (2) oak gall (an ingredient in ink)

11   *goose-pen*
A quill pen made from a goose feather. The goose was thought to be a particularly meek and cowardly bird.

banged the youth into dumbness. This was looked for   20
neglected   at your hand, [1] and this was balked.° The double gilt of
this opportunity [2] you let time wash off, and you are
now sailed into the north of my lady's opinion, [3] where
you will hang like an icicle on a Dutchman's beard, [4]
unless you do redeem it by some laudable attempt   25
strategy   either of valor or policy.°

Sir Andrew

If   An° 't be any way, it must be with valor, for policy I
willingly   hate. I had as lief° be a Brownist [5] as a politician.

Sir Toby Belch

Why, then, build me [6] thy fortunes upon the basis of
valor. Challenge me the Count's youth to fight with   30
him. Hurt him in eleven places. My niece shall take
note of it, and, assure thyself, there is no love-broker
in the world can more prevail in man's commendation
with woman than report of valor.

Fabian

There is no way but this, Sir Andrew.   35

Sir Andrew

Will either of you bear me a challenge to him?

Sir Toby Belch

angry   Go; write it in a martial hand. Be curst° and brief. It is
no matter how witty, so it be eloquent and full of
invention. Taunt him with the license of ink. [7] If thou
"thou"-est [8] him some thrice, it shall not be amiss; and   40
accusations of lying   as many lies° as will lie in thy sheet of paper, although
the sheet were big enough for the bed of Ware [9] in
England, set 'em down. Go; about it. Let there be gall [10]
enough in thy ink, though thou write with a goose-
pen, [11] no matter. About it.   45

Sir Andrew

Where shall I find you?

1 *dear manikin*

    I.e., enjoyable plaything (Toby
    puns on a different sense of *dear*
    (expensive) in the following line.)

2 *Never trust me, then.*

    Never trust me again (if I fail to
    deliver the letter).

3 *blood in his liver*

    The lack of blood in the liver was
    thought to be a sign of cowardice.

4 *youngest wren*

    The smallest of a brood of small
    birds; another reference to Maria's
    small stature.

5 *desire the spleen*

    I.e., wish to laugh heartily (the
    spleen was thought to be the seat
    of laughter)

6 renegado

    Spanish term for a Christian who
    has converted to Islam. Maria uses
    the term to describe the radical
    transformation of Malvolio's
    behavior.

7 *impossible passages of grossness*

    Unbelievably outrageous
    statements (that were written in
    the false letter).

Sir Toby Belch

bed chamber   We'll call thee at the cubiculo.° Go.

Sir Andrew *exits.*

Fabian

This is a dear manikin [1] to you, Sir Toby.

Sir Toby Belch

costly / i.e., ducats   I have been dear° to him, lad, some two thousand°
strong or so.   50

Fabian

extraordinary   We shall have a rare° letter from him. But you'll not
deliver 't?

Sir Toby Belch

urge   Never trust me, then. [2] And by all means stir° on the
wagon ropes   youth to an answer. I think oxen and wainropes° cannot
pull   hale° them together. For Andrew, if he were opened   55
weigh down   and you find so much blood in his liver [3] as will clog°
cadaver   the foot of a flea, I'll eat the rest of th' anatomy.°

Fabian

adversary / face   And his opposite,° the youth, bears in his visage° no
great presage of cruelty.

Enter **Maria**.

Sir Toby Belch

Look where the youngest wren [4] of mine comes.   60

Maria

If you desire the spleen [5] and will laugh yourself into
fool   stitches, follow me. Yond gull° Malvolio is turned hea-
then, a very *renegado*, [6] for there is no Christian that
who could   means to be saved by believing rightly can° ever believe
such impossible passages of grossness. [7] He's in yellow   65
stockings!

1 *that keeps a school i' the church*

A community too small to have a
dedicated schoolhouse would
have held classes in its church
building. Such communities were
often poor, remote, or both, and
therefore unlikely to attract any
but the least qualified teachers.

2 *the new map with the augmentation of*
   the Indies

In 1599, a map by Emmeric
Mollineux was published showing
the East Indies in greater detail
than any previous one. This map
(the *augmentation*) used many more
projection lines than most earlier
maps, hence the comparison with
the wrinkles produced by
Malvolio's smile.

Sir Toby Belch

And cross-gartered?

Maria

abominably / teacher   Most villanously,° like a pedant° that keeps a school
i' th' church. [1] I have dogged him like his murderer. He
does obey every point of the letter that I dropped to   70
betray him. He does smile his face into more lines than
is in the new map with the augmentation of the Indies. [2]
You have not seen such a thing as 'tis. I can hardly
keep from   forbear° hurling things at him. I know my lady will
strike him. If she do, he'll smile and take 't for a great   75
favor.

Sir Toby Belch

Come; bring us, bring us where he is.   *They all exit.*

1 *by my will*

Intentionally

2 *filèd*

Sharpened (by filing)

3 *not all love*

Not merely the desire

4 *The rather by these arguments of fear*

More speedily because of these concerns

5 *oft good turns / Are shuffled off with such uncurrent pay*

I.e., often good deeds are acknowledged with nothing more than similarly empty words

6 *relics*

Antiquities (i.e., tourist sights)

Act 3, Scene 3

Enter **Sebastian** *and* **Antonio**.

Sebastian

I would not by my will¹ have troubled you,
But, since you make your pleasure of your pains,
I will no further chide you.

Antonio

I could not stay behind you. My desire,
More sharp than filèd² steel, did spur me forth,   5
And not all love³ to see you, though so much
As might have drawn one to a longer voyage,

fear for   But jealousy° what might befall your travel,
inexperienced   Being skilless° in these parts, which to a stranger,
Unguided and unfriended, often prove   10
Rough and unhospitable. My willing love,
The rather by these arguments of fear,⁴
Set forth in your pursuit.

Sebastian

               My kind Antonio,
I can no other answer make but thanks,

continued   And thanks, and ever° thanks—and oft good turns   15
worthless   Are shuffled off with such uncurrent° pay.⁵
wealth   But were my worth,° as is my conscience, firm,
You should find better dealing. What's to do?
Shall we go see the relics⁶ of this town?

Antonio

Tomorrow, sir. Best first go see your lodging.   20

Sebastian

I am not weary, and 'tis long to night.
I pray you, let us satisfy our eyes
With the memorials and the things of fame

make famous   That do renown° this city.

1   *Count his*

    Count's (i.e., Orsino's)

2   *it would scarce be answered*

    **Either (1) it would be difficult for
me to make reparations (because I
lack the necessary funds); or (2) it
would be difficult to defend myself
in the eyes of the law. By staying in
Illyria, Antonio puts his life in
danger.**

3   *quality of the time*

    Circumstances at the time

4   *bloody argument*

    **A dispute worth shedding blood
over**

5   *for traffic's sake*

    **In order to reestablish favorable
trade relations**

6   *It doth not fit me.*

    It's not appropriate for me to do so.

7   *Elephant*

    The name of an inn

8   *bespeak our diet*

    Order our meals

9   *not for idle markets*

    Insufficient for buying luxury items

Antonio

   I wish   Would° you'd pardon me;

                   I do not without danger walk these streets.   25

   ships   Once in a sea-fight 'gainst the Count his [1] galleys°

 prominence   I did some service, of such note° indeed

  captured   That were I ta'en° here it would scarce be answered. [2]

Sebastian

 I suppose   Belike° you slew great number of his people.

Antonio

          Th' offence is not of such a bloody nature,   30

          Albeit the quality of the time [3] and quarrel

          Might well have given us bloody argument. [4]

  satisfied   It might have since been answered° in repaying

          What we took from them, which, for traffic's sake, [5]

          Most of our city did. Only myself stood out,   35

   caught   For which, if I be lapsèd° in this place,

   dearly   I shall pay dear.°

Sebastian

                  Do not then walk too open.

Antonio

          It doth not fit me. [6] Hold, sir, here's my purse.

          In the south suburbs, at the Elephant, [7]

          Is best to lodge. I will bespeak our diet, [8]   40

i.e., pleasantly pass Whiles you beguile° the time and feed your knowledge

    find   With viewing of the town. There shall you have° me.

Sebastian

          Why I your purse?

Antonio

Perhaps / trifle Haply° your eye shall light upon some toy°

supply (of cash) You have desire to purchase, and your store,°   45

          I think, is not for idle markets, [9] sir.

Sebastian

I'll be your purse-bearer and leave you
For an hour.

Antonio

       To th' Elephant.

Sebastian

            I do remember.

They exit [in different directions].

1   *He says he'll come.*

    **Olivia is anticipating Cesario's
    response and then worrying about
    how effectively to "greet" him.**

2   *sad and civil*

    Grave and deferential

3   *sure possessed*

    Surely possessed (by the devil)

4   *upon a sad occasion*

    Regarding a serious issue

Act 3, Scene 4

Enter **Olivia** *and* **Maria**.

Olivia

i.e., Cesario [*aside*] I have sent after him.° He says he'll come.[1]

on How shall I feast him? What bestow of° him?

For youth is bought more oft than begged or borrowed.

I speak too loud.

[*to* **Maria**] Where's Malvolio?—He is sad and civil[2]   5

And suits well for a servant with my fortunes.

—Where is Malvolio?

Maria

He's coming, madam, but in very strange manner. He is

sure possessed,[3] madam.

Olivia

talk wildly Why, what's the matter? Does he rave?°   10

Maria

No, madam; he does nothing but smile. Your Ladyship

were best to have some guard about you if he come, for

sure the man is tainted in 's wits.

Olivia

Go call him hither.   [**Maria** *exits.*]

lunatic   I am as mad° as he,

If sad and merry madness equal be.   15

Enter [**Maria**, *with*] **Malvolio**.

How now, Malvolio?

Malvolio

Sweet lady, ho, ho.

Olivia

Smil'st thou? I sent for thee upon a sad occasion.[4]

1   *"Please one, and please all."*

I.e., "pleasing one woman is as
good as pleasing them all." The
line comes from a popular bawdy
song of the period.

2   *Not black in my mind, though yellow in
my legs.*

I.e., I'm not melancholy, though I
wear yellow stockings on my legs.

3   *sweet Roman hand*

Fashionable italic handwriting (as
opposed to the familiar English
"secretary" style)

4   *go to bed*

I.e., in order to recuperate through
bed rest. Malvolio understands
Olivia's line as a sexual invitation.

5   *"Ay, sweetheart, and I'll come to thee."*

A line from a popular ballad

6   *At your request? Yes, nightingales
answer daws!*

I.e., you expect me to respond to
you? I suppose so, since even
(sweet singing) nightingales sing
in response to (croaking)
jackdaws!

Malvolio

Sad, lady? I could be sad. This does make some obstruction in the blood, this cross-gartering, but what of   20
that? If it please the eye of one, it is with me as the very
song   true sonnet° is: "Please one, and please all." [1]

Olivia

Why, how dost thou, man? What is the matter with
thee?

Malvolio

i.e., the letter   Not black in my mind, though yellow in my legs. [2] It° did   25
come to his hands, and commands shall be executed. I
think we do know the sweet Roman hand. [3]

Olivia

Wilt thou go to bed, [4] Malvolio?

Malvolio

To bed? "Ay, sweetheart, and I'll come to thee." [5]

Olivia

God comfort thee! Why dost thou smile so and kiss thy   30
hand so oft?

Maria

How do you, Malvolio?

Malvolio

At your request? Yes, nightingales answer daws! [6]

Maria

Why appear you with this ridiculous boldness before
my lady?   35

Malvolio

"Be not afraid of greatness." 'Twas well writ.

Olivia

What mean'st thou by that, Malvolio?

Malvolio

"Some are born great—"

1 *very midsummer madness*

I.e., true insanity (the summer
moon was thought to cause
lunacy)

Olivia

Ha?

Malvolio

"Some achieve greatness—"   40

Olivia

What say'st thou?

Malvolio

"And some have greatness thrust upon them."

Olivia

Heaven restore thee!

Malvolio

"Remember who commended thy yellow stockings—"

Olivia

Thy yellow stockings?   45

Malvolio

"And wished to see thee cross-gartered."

Olivia

Cross-gartered?

Malvolio

"Go to, thou art made, if thou desir'st to be so—"

Olivia

Am I made?

Malvolio

"If not, let me see thee a servant still."   50

Olivia

Why, this is very midsummer madness. [1]

Enter **Servant**.

Servant

Madam, the young gentleman of the Count Orsino's is
returned. I could hardly entreat him back. He attends
your Ladyship's pleasure.

1 *come near me*

   Properly appreciate me

2 *in the habit of some sir of note*

   Dressed like a nobleman

3 *limed*

   I.e., caught. Lime, a sticky substance, was used to trap small birds.

4 *Jove's doing*

   I.e., god's achievement. In Roman mythology, Jove was the king of the gods.

5 *Fellow*

   The word *fellow* could be used dismissively or patronizingly to refer to a person of inferior rank, but Malvolio imagines that Olivia has used the word in a more intimate sense to mean "companion" or "partner."

6 *after my degree*

   According to my rank (as Olivia's steward)

7 *no dram of a scruple, no scruple of a scruple*

   I.e., not even the slightest doubt. A *dram* is one eighth of a fluid ounce; a *scruple* is both one third of a dram, and "a doubt or uncertainty."

Olivia

I'll come to him.   [*The* **Servant** *exits.*]   55

Good Maria, let this fellow be looked to. Where's my

cousin Toby? Let some of my people have a special care

be harmed   of him. I would not have him miscarry° for the half of

my dowry.   [**Olivia** *and* **Maria**] *exit.*

Malvolio

Oh, ho! Do you come near me ¹ now? No worse man   60

than Sir Toby to look to me! This concurs directly with

the letter. She sends him on purpose that I may appear

stubborn to him, for she incites me to that in the let-

ter. "Cast thy humble slough," says she. "Be opposite

with a kinsman, surly with servants. Let thy tongue   65

tang with arguments of state. Put thyself into the trick

subsequently   of singularity," and consequently° sets down the

somber / grave   manner how: as, a sad° face, a reverend° carriage, a

slow tongue, in the habit of some sir of note, ² and so

forth. I have limed ³ her, but it is Jove's doing, ⁴ and Jove   70

make me thankful! And when she went away now, "Let

this fellow be looked to." "Fellow!" ⁵ Not "Malvolio,"

nor after my degree, ⁶ but "fellow." Why, everything

so that   adheres together, that° no dram of a scruple, no scruple

incredible / unreliable   of a scruple, ⁷ no obstacle, no incredulous° or unsafe°   75

circumstance—what can be said?—nothing that can

be can come between me and the full prospect of my

hopes. Well, Jove, not I, is the doer of this, and he is to

be thanked.

Enter [**Sir**] **Toby** [**Belch**], **Fabian**, *and* **Maria**.

1   *drawn in little*

   Gathered together in one small
   area (i.e., inside Malvolio)

2   *Legion himself*

   I.e., a demon. Mark 5:9 in the New
   Testament describes how an
   "unclean spirit" once possessed
   the soul of an unfortunate man.
   When Jesus asked the spirit's
   name, he answered: "My name is
   Legion, for we are many" (*legion*
   meaning "innumerable").

3   *how hollow the fiend speaks within him*

   Maria attributes Malvolio's
   pretention to the devil inhabiting
   his body and speaking falsely
   (*hollow*) through him, or perhaps
   merely comments on his booming
   dismissal, *Go off*.

4   *Let me alone.*

   I.e., let me handle him by myself.

5   *Carry his water to th' wise woman.*

   Bring his urine to the healer (for
   diagnosis of his sickness).

Sir Toby Belch

Which way is he, in the name of sanctity? If all the   80
devils of hell be drawn in little, [1] and Legion himself[2]
possessed him, yet I'll speak to him.

Fabian

Here he is; here he is.—How is 't with you, sir? How is
't with you, man?

Malvolio

privacy Go off; I discard you. Let me enjoy my private.° Go off.   85

Maria

Lo, how hollow the fiend speaks within him! [3] Did not
I tell you? Sir Toby, my lady prays you to have a care of
him.

Malvolio

Aha! Does she so?

Sir Toby Belch

[to **Fabian** and **Maria**] Go to, go to! Peace, peace. We   90
must deal gently with him. Let me alone. [4]—How do
you, Malvolio? How is 't with you? What, man, defy the
devil! Consider, he's an enemy to mankind.

Malvolio

Do you know what you say?

Maria

Look/if [to **Sir Toby Belch**] La° you, an° you speak ill of the   95
to devil, how he takes it at° heart! Pray God he be not
bewitched!

Fabian

Carry his water to th' wise woman. [5]

Maria

Marry, and it shall be done tomorrow morning if I live.
My lady would not lose him for more than I'll say.   100

Malvolio

How now, mistress?

1   *bawcock*

I.e., good sir (From the French *beau coq*, or handsome bird); *bawcock*, *chuck* (in line 3.4.108), and *biddy* (in 3.4.110) are all similar terms of endearment.

2   *for gravity*

Fit for a man of dignity

3   *play at cherry-pit*

I.e., be familiar with. *Cherry-pit* is a children's game of tossing cherry pits into a hole.

4   *foul collier*

Filthy coal man (here referring to Satan)

Maria

O Lord!

Sir Toby Belch

[*to* **Maria**] Prithee, hold thy peace. This is not the way. Do

upset you not see you move° him? Let me alone with him.

Fabian

No way but gentleness—gently, gently. The fiend is   105

violent / treated rough° and will not be roughly used.°

Sir Toby Belch

[*to* **Malvolio**] Why, how now, my bawcock!¹ How dost

chick thou, chuck?°

Malvolio

Sir!

Sir Toby Belch

chick Ay, biddy,° come with me.—What, man! 'Tis not for   110

gravity² to play at cherry-pit³ with Satan. Hang him,

foul collier!⁴

Maria

Get him to say his prayers, good Sir Toby; get him to

pray.

Malvolio

brazen woman My prayers, minx?°   115

Maria

[*to* **Sir Toby Belch**] No, I warrant you, he will not hear

of godliness.

Malvolio

foolish Go, hang yourselves all! You are idle,° shallow things. I am

social sphere not of your element.° You shall know more hereafter.

He exits.

Sir Toby Belch

Is 't possible?   120

1   *genius*

    Guardian spirit

2   *take air and taint*

    **I.e., be discovered and therefore
    ruined. The metaphor is drawn
    from food, which spoils (*taints*) if
    left out in the open *air*.**

3   *in a dark room and bound*

    **I.e., put in a cell and tied up (a
    common treatment for insanity in
    Shakespeare's day)**

4   *bring the device to the bar*

    I.e., take the scheme into open court

5   *matter for a May morning*

    **Amusement suitable for a holiday
    (May Day)**

6   *saucy*

    **Insolent or defiant, but punning
    on *saucy* meaning "seasoned" (with
    vinegar and pepper.)**

7   *I warrant him*

    **I guarantee it (in Shakespeare's
    time *him* could be used as a neuter
    pronoun), but perhaps "I can
    assure him" (refering to Cesario).**

Fabian

If this were played upon a stage now, I could condemn
it as an improbable fiction.

Sir Toby Belch

plot   His very genius[1] hath taken the infection of the device,°
man.

Maria

Nay, pursue him now, lest the device take air and taint.[2]   125

Fabian

Why, we shall make him mad indeed.

Maria

The house will be the quieter.

Sir Toby Belch

Come; we'll have him in a dark room and bound.[3] My
niece is already in the belief that he's mad. We may
continue   carry° it thus, for our pleasure and his penance, till our   130
very pastime, tired out of breath, prompt us to have
mercy on him, at which time we will bring the device to
as   the bar[4] and crown thee for° a finder of madmen. But
see, but see!

Enter **Sir Andrew**.

Fabian

More matter for a May morning.[5]   135

Sir Andrew

[*offering a paper*] Here's the challenge; read it. I warrant
there's vinegar and pepper in 't.

Fabian

Is 't so saucy?[6]

Sir Andrew

Ay, is 't, I warrant him.[7] Do but read.

1   *that keeps you from the blow of the law*

    **Prevents you from being arrested
    (for libel)**

2   *thou liest in thy throat*

    **I.e., you lie completely. Note also
    that Sir Andrew has taken Sir Toby's
    advice to use the insulting *thou* (see
    3.2.40 and note).**

3   *windy side*

    **Windward side (that side from which
    the wind is blowing; i.e., the safe side)**

Sir Toby Belch

Give me. [*reads*] "Youth, whatsoever thou art, thou art 140

despicable but a scurvy° fellow."

Fabian

Good, and valiant.

Sir Toby Belch

marvel [*reads*] "Wonder not, nor admire° not in thy mind, why I

do call thee so, for I will show thee no reason for 't."

Fabian

A good note; that keeps you from the blow of the law. [1] 145

Sir Toby Belch

opinion [*reads*] "Thou com'st to the Lady Olivia, and in my sight°

treats she uses° thee kindly. But thou liest in thy throat. [2] That

is not the matter I challenge thee for."

Fabian

Very brief, and to exceeding good sense—[*aside*] less.

Sir Toby Belch

[*reads*] "I will waylay thee going home, where if it be thy 150

chance to kill me—"

Fabian

Good.

Sir Toby Belch

[*reads*] "Thou kill'st me like a rogue and a villain."

Fabian

Still you keep o' th' windy side [3] of the law. Good.

Sir Toby Belch

[*reads*] "Fare thee well, and God have mercy upon one of 155

our souls. He may have mercy upon mine, but my hope

after is better, and so look to° thyself. Thy friend, as thou

usest him, and thy sworn enemy, Andrew Aguecheek."

upset If this letter move° him not, his legs cannot. I'll give 't

him. 160

1   *Scout me*

    Look (*me* is an intensifier as at
    3.2.29 and 30 and note)

2   *bum-baily*

    A derogatory colloquialism for a
    bailiff (a minor officer of the law).

3   *proof*

    Trial; an actual demonstration

4   *let me alone for swearing*

    Leave the cursing to me; don't
    worry about my ability to swear.

5   *gives him out to be*

    Demonstrates that he is

6   *as I know his youth will aptly receive it*

    As I know, since he's young, that he
    will readily accept it

7   *cockatrices*

    Mythical creatures that could kill
    with looks.

8   *Give them way*

    Stay out of their way.

Maria

You may have very fit occasion for 't. He is now in some

conversation commerce° with my lady and will by and by depart.

Sir Toby Belch

Go, Sir Andrew. Scout me[1] for him at the corner of the

orchard like a bum-baily.[2] So soon as ever thou see'st

horribly him, draw, and as thou draw'st, swear horrible,° for it   165

comes to pass oft that a terrible oath, with a swagger-

ing accent sharply twanged off, gives manhood more

credit approbation° than ever proof[3] itself would have earned

him. Away!

Sir Andrew

Nay, let me alone for swearing.[4]   *He exits.*   170

Sir Toby Belch

Now will not I deliver his letter, for the behavior of the

i.e., intellect young gentleman gives him out to be[5] of good capacity°

and breeding. His employment between his lord and

my niece confirms no less. Therefore this letter, being

so excellently ignorant, will breed no terror in the   175

idiot youth. He will find it comes from a clodpole.° But, sir, I

place will deliver his challenge by word of mouth, set° upon

Aguecheek a notable report of valor, and drive the gen-

tleman (as I know his youth will aptly receive it[6]) into a

terrifying most hideous° opinion of his rage, skill, fury, and   180

impetuosity. This will so fright them both that they will

kill one another by the look, like cockatrices.[7]

Enter **Olivia** *and* **Viola**.

Fabian

Here he comes with your niece. Give them way[8] till he

immediately (go) take leave and presently° after him.

1   *laid mine honor too unchary on 't*

    **Risked my reputation too
    recklessly for it**

2   *With the same 'havior that your passion
    bears*

    **In the same manner that marks
    your love**

3   *jewel*

    **I.e., piece of jewelry (a locket with
    a miniature painting of Olivia)**

4   *That honor, saved, may upon asking give*

    **That honor may agree to grant
    without damaging itself**

5   *I will acquit you.*

    **I.e., I will release you from your
    vows.**

Sir Toby Belch

frightening   I will meditate the while upon some horrid° message   185

for a challenge.

[**Sir Toby Belch**, **Fabian**, _and_ **Maria** _exit_.]

Olivia

I have said too much unto a heart of stone

And laid mine honor too unchary on 't. [1]

admonishes   There's something in me that reproves° my fault,

But such a headstrong potent fault it is   190

merely   That it but° mocks reproof.

Viola

With the same 'havior that your passion bears [2]

Goes on my master's grief.

Olivia

Here; wear this jewel [3] for me. 'Tis my picture.

i.e., voice   Refuse it not; it hath no tongue° to vex you.   195

And I beseech you come again tomorrow.

What shall you ask of me that I'll deny,

That honor, saved, may upon asking give? [4]

Viola

Nothing but this: your true love for my master.

Olivia

How with mine honor may I give him that   200

Which I have given to you?

Viola

                 I will acquit you. [5]

Olivia

Well, come again tomorrow. Fare thee well.

A fiend like thee might bear my soul to hell.   [_She exits_.]

Enter [**Sir**] **Toby** [**Belch**] _and_ **Fabian**.

1   *That defense thou hast, betake thee to 't.*

Whatever defensive abilities you possess, get ready to use them.

2   *thy intercepter*

I.e., he who would encounter you

3   *Dismount thy tuck*

Draw your sword

4   *dubbed with unhatched rapier*

With a knighthood conferred with an unused sword (i.e., at court rather than on the battlefield)

5   *on carpet consideration*

I.e., for non-military services to the court (i.e., the knighthood was purchased not earned)

6   *Souls and bodies hath he divorced three*

I.e., he has killed three people

7   *satisfaction can be none but by*

He can only be satisfied by

8   *"Hob nob"*

Have or have not (i.e., "it's all the same to me"); the following phrase, *give't or take't*, is essentially a paraphrase.

9   *put quarrels purposely on*

Purposely pick fights with

Sir Toby Belch

Gentleman, God save thee.

Viola

And you, sir.   205

Sir Toby Belch

That defense thou hast, betake thee to 't.[1] Of what
nature the wrongs are thou hast done him, I know not,

malice   but thy intercepter,[2] full of despite,° bloody as the
waits for   hunter, attends° thee at the orchard end. Dismount thy
quick   tuck,[3] be yare° in thy preparation, for thy assailant is   210
quick, skillful, and deadly.

Viola

with   You mistake, sir. I am sure no man hath any quarrel to°
memory me. My remembrance° is very free and clear from any
image of offense done to any man.

Sir Toby Belch

You'll find it otherwise, I assure you. Therefore, if you   215

value   hold your life at any price,° betake you to your guard,
opponent for your opposite° hath in him what youth, strength,
with   skill, and wrath can furnish man withal.°

Viola

I pray you, sir, what is he?

Sir Toby Belch

He is knight, dubbed with unhatched rapier[4] and on   220
carpet consideration,[5] but he is a devil in private brawl.
Souls and bodies hath he divorced three,[6] and his

rage   incensement° at this moment is so implacable that satisfaction can be none but by[7] pangs of death and sepulchre.

motto   "Hob nob"[8] is his word;° give 't or take 't.   225

Viola

I will return again into the house and desire some
i.e., safe passage conduct° of the lady. I am no fighter. I have heard of
some kind of men that put quarrels purposely on[9] others,

1   *a very competent injury*

     **A wrong that definitely requires a
     response.**

2   *forswear to wear iron about you*

     **Never again wear a sword (i.e.,
     admit that you're a coward)**

3   *know of*

     Learn from

4   *a mortal arbitrament*

     A deadly confrontation

5   *Nothing of that wonderful promise, to
     read him by his form, as you are like to
     find him in the proof of his valor.*

     **Not as remarkable in his outward
     appearance as you will find him
     when he demonstrates his bravery.**

6   *Will you*

     If you will

test / Perhaps / habit   to taste° their valor. Belike° this is a man of that quirk.°

Sir Toby Belch

Sir, no. His indignation derives itself out of a very com-   230
petent injury;[1] therefore get you on and give him his
desire. Back you shall not to the house, unless you

i.e., a duel   undertake that° with me which with as much safety

i.e., fight with   you might answer° him. Therefore on, or strip your

fight   sword stark naked; for meddle° you must, that's cer-   235
tain, or forswear to wear iron about you.[2]

Viola

This is as uncivil as strange. I beseech you, do me this

service   courteous office° as to know of[3] the knight what my
offense to him is. It is something of my negligence,

intention   nothing of my purpose.°   240

Sir Toby Belch

I will do so. Signior Fabian, stay you by this gentleman
till my return.   *He exits.*

Viola

Pray you, sir, do you know of this matter?

Fabian

I know the knight is incensed against you, even to a
mortal arbitrament,[4] but nothing of the circumstance   245
more.

Viola

I beseech you, what manner of man is he?

Fabian

judge   Nothing of that wonderful promise, to read° him by his

likely   form, as you are like° to find him in the proof of his
valor.[5] He is, indeed, sir, the most skillful, bloody, and   250

opponent   fatal opposite° that you could possibly have found in
any part of Illyria. Will you[6] walk towards him, I will
make your peace with him if I can.

1 They exit.

The usually reliable Folio text of the play has Fabian and Cesario exit here, requiring their reentry after line 272. The convention of a clear stage usually indicates a change of scene, yet this one is continuous. Sir Toby's claim that Fabian can barely restrain Cesario *yonder* (265) suggests that the audience can see some activity between Fabian and Cesario, such as Fabian struggling to keep Cesario from fleeing. On an Elizabethan stage, with two doors on the back wall of the stage, Viola and Fabian could presumably still be seen in the doorway through which they had exited, or perhaps could be glimpsed tussling behind a curtain. Sir Toby and Andrew enter through the second door and move downstage so as to be in Cesario's sight line, so that the antagonists are in opposite corners, like boxers. Sir Toby and Fabian can then leave their charges and meet in the middle, then return and urge them toward each other so that they are facing off in center stage when Antonio enters after line 291.

2 *virago*

A female warrior. Toby is not suggesting that Cesario is a woman, merely that his youth gives him a feminine aspect.

3 *stuck-in*

Thrust; a fencing move (from the Italian *stoccata*)

4 *I have his horse to take up the quarrel.*

I have the promise of his horse to settle the quarrel (see lines 302–303).

Viola

I shall be much bound to you for 't. I am one that had
rather go with Sir Priest than Sir Knight. I care not who   *255*
character   knows so much of my mettle.°   *They exit.* ¹

Enter [**Sir**] **Toby** [**Belch**], *and* [**Sir**] **Andrew**.

Sir Toby Belch

Why, man, he's a very devil. I have not seen such a
bout   virago. ² I had a pass° with him, rapier, scabbard, and all,
deadly   and he gives me the stuck-in ³ with such a mortal°
return blow motion that it is inevitable. And on the answer,° he   *260*
kills   pays° you as surely as your feet hits the ground they step
Shah of Persia   on. They say he has been fencer to the Sophy.°

Sir Andrew

Pox on 't! I'll not meddle with him.

Sir Toby Belch

Ay, but he will not now be pacified. Fabian can scarce
hold him yonder.   *265*

Sir Andrew

If   Plague on 't! An° I thought he had been valiant and so
fencing   cunning in fence,° I'd have seen him damned ere I'd
have challenged him. Let him let the matter slip, and
I'll give him my horse, gray Capilet.

Sir Toby Belch

proposal   I'll make the motion.° Stand here; make a good show   *270*
loss/i.e., life   on 't. This shall end without the perdition° of souls.°
[*aside*] Marry, I'll ride your horse as well as I ride you.

Enter **Fabian** *and* **Viola**.

[*aside to* **Fabian**] I have his horse to take up the quarrel. ⁴

1   *He is as horribly conceited of him*

    I.e., Cesario holds the same terrifying thoughts about Sir Andrew.

2   *he hath better bethought him of his quarrel*

    He has reconsidered the thing he was upset about (i.e., the insult he claimed you leveled at him).

3   *for the supportance of his vow*

    In order that he might uphold the promise he made (to fight you)

4   *A little thing would make me tell them how much I lack of a man.*

    I'm very close to admitting what a coward I truly am (with a sexual joke on *the little thing*, or penis, which Viola does, of course, *lack*).

5   *Give ground if you see him furious.*

    Retreat if he loses his temper.

6   *the* duello

    The rules of dueling

I have persuaded him the youth's a devil.

Fabian

He is as horribly conceited of him, [1] and pants and   275
looks pale, as if a bear were at his heels.

Sir Toby Belch

[*to* **Viola**] There's no remedy, sir. He will fight with you
for 's oath sake. Marry, he hath better bethought him
of his quarrel, [2] and he finds that now scarce to be
worth talking of. Therefore, draw for the supportance   280
of his vow. [3] He protests he will not hurt you.

Viola

[*aside*] Pray God defend me! A little thing would make
me tell them how much I lack of a man. [4]

Fabian

Give ground if you see him furious. [5]

Sir Toby Belch

Come, Sir Andrew; there's no remedy. The gentleman   285
will, for his honor's sake, have one bout with you. He
cannot by the *duello* [6] avoid it. But he has promised me,
as he is a gentleman and a soldier, he will not hurt you.
Come on; to 't.

Sir Andrew

Pray God he keep his oath!   290

Viola

I do assure you, 'tis against my will.   [*They draw swords.*]

Enter **Antonio**.

Antonio

i.e., Cesario Put up your sword. If this young gentleman°
Have done offense, I take the fault on me.
If you offend him, I for him defy you.

1 *undertaker*

Someone who would undertake to
fight (i.e., a challenger)

2 *for that*

As for that which

3 *He*

I.e., Sir Andrew's horse Capilet,
which Sir Andrew promised to give
to Cesario (line 269)

4 *no jot*

Not at all

Sir Toby Belch

You, sir? Why, what are you?   295

Antonio

One, sir, that for his love dares yet do more

Than you have heard him brag to you he will.

Sir Toby Belch

i.e., ready for   Nay, if you be an undertaker, [1] I am for° you.

[*They draw their swords.*]

Enter **Officers**.

Fabian

O good Sir Toby, hold! Here come the officers.

Sir Toby Belch

shortly   [*to* **Antonio**] I'll be with you anon.°   300

Viola

[*to* **Sir Andrew**] Pray, sir, put your sword up, if you please.

Sir Andrew

Marry, will I, sir, and for that[2] I promised you, I'll be as

good as my word. He[3] will bear you easily and reins well.

First Officer

This is the man. Do thy office.

Second Officer

Antonio, I arrest thee at the suit of Count Orsino.   305

Antonio

You do mistake me, sir.

First Officer

face   No, sir, no jot.[4] I know your favor° well,

Though now you have no sea-cap on your head.

—Take him away. He knows I know him well.

Antonio

as a result of   I must obey. [*to* **Viola**] This comes with° seeking you.   310

answer for   But there's no remedy; I shall answer° it.

1   *I'll make division of my present with you*

   **I'll give you a portion of the money
I have now.**

2   *Hold*

   **I.e., hold out your hand (or maybe
merely "wait," as Antonio perhaps
turns away in anger at what he
takes as ingratitude)**

3   *coffer*

   **Chest of money; referring here to
her purse**

4   *Is 't possible that my deserts to you / Can
lack persuasion?*

   **Is it possible that the deserving
service I've done for you can fail to
persuade you (to give me money)?**

What will you do, now my necessity

Makes me to ask you for my purse? It grieves me

Much more for what I cannot do for you

bewildered   Than what befalls myself. You stand amazed,°   315

But be of comfort.

Second Officer

Come, sir, away.

Antonio

[*to* **Viola**] I must entreat of you some of that money.

Viola

What money, sir?

For the fair kindness you have showed me here,   320

i.e., in part   And part° being prompted by your present trouble,

Out of my lean and low ability

fortune   I'll lend you something. My having° is not much;

I'll make division of my present with you. [1]

Hold; [2] there's half my coffer. [3] [*hands him money*]

Antonio

                       Will you deny me now?   325

Is 't possible that my deserts to you

Can lack persuasion? [4] Do not tempt my misery,

wicked   Lest that it make me so unsound° a man

reproach   As to upbraid° you with those kindnesses

That I have done for you.

Viola

                   I know of none,   330

Nor know I you by voice or any feature.

I hate ingratitude more in a man

Than lying, vainness, babbling drunkenness,

Or any taint of vice whose strong corruption

nature   Inhabits our frail blood°—

Antonio

                 O heavens themselves!   335

1   *one half out of the jaws of death*

    I.e., half dead

2   *which methought did promise / Most*
    venerable worth

    Which I thought was worthy of
    being venerated

3   *done good feature shame*

    Disgraced your considerable beauty

4   *In nature there's no blemish but the mind*

    Nothing natural can be ugly,
    except for flaws of character.

5   *unkind*

    (1) unsympathetic or ungrateful;
    (2) unnatural

6   *empty trunks o'erflourished by the devil*

    Empty boxes elaborately
    decorated by the devil (to seem
    beautiful and valuable)

7   *So do not I.*

    I.e., I don't believe him. However,
    the sense may be closer to "I would
    like to believe him but I don't dare"
    (since it might mean Sebastian is
    alive).

Second Officer

Come, sir; I pray you, go.

Antonio

Let me speak a little. This youth that you see here
I snatched one half out of the jaws of death,[1]

devotion   Relieved him with such sanctity° of love,

appearance   And to his image,° which methought did promise   *340*

acts of worship   Most venerable worth,[2] did I devotion.°

First Officer

What's that to us? The time goes by. Away!

Antonio

But, oh, how vile an idol proves this god!
Thou hast, Sebastian, done good feature shame.[3]
In nature there's no blemish but the mind:[4]   *345*
None can be called deformed but the unkind.[5]
Virtue is beauty, but the beauteous evil
Are empty trunks o'erflourished by the devil.[6]

First Officer

The man grows mad. Away with him. Come, come, sir.

Antonio

Lead me on.   *350*

*He exits [with the **Officers**].*

Viola

intense emontion   Methinks his words do from such passion° fly
That he believes himself. So do not I.[7]
Prove true, imagination, oh, prove true,
That I, dear brother, be now ta'en for you!

Sir Toby Belch

Come hither, knight. Come hither, Fabian. We'll whisper   *355*

maxims   o'er a couplet or two of most sage saws.°

[**Sir Toby Belch**, **Sir Andrew**, *and* **Fabian** *move away*.]

1   *I my brother know / Yet living in my glass.*

    **I can always see my brother when I
    look into the mirror.**

2   *Even such and so / In favor*

    In exactly this appearance

3   *religious in it*

    **Completely devoted to it (i.e.,
    cowardice)**

4   *'twill be nothing yet*

    It won't amount to anything after all

Viola

He named Sebastian. I my brother know

Always   Yet° living in my glass.¹ Even such and so

In favor² was my brother, and he went

Always   Still° in this fashion, color, ornament,   360

prove true For him I imitate. Oh, if it prove,°

Tempests are kind and salt waves fresh in love!

[*She exits.*]

Sir Toby Belch

dishonorable A very dishonest° paltry boy, and more a coward than a

hare. His dishonesty appears in leaving his friend here

in necessity and denying him; and for his cowardship,   365

ask Fabian.

Fabian

A coward, a most devout coward, religious in it.³

Sir Andrew

By God's eyelid 'Slid,° I'll after him again and beat him.

Sir Toby Belch

Do, cuff him soundly, but never draw thy sword.

Sir Andrew

If   An° I do not—   [*He exits.*] 370

Fabian

outcome Come, let's see the event.°

Sir Toby Belch

I dare lay any money 'twill be nothing yet.⁴   *They exit.*

1   *Will you*

    Are you trying to

2   *held out*

    Kept up

3   *ungird thy strangeness*

    Take off your remoteness; i.e., quit acting like you don't know me. Feste mocks Sebastian's formality by speaking in similarly elevated language.

4   *foolish Greek*

    I.e., buffoon ("merry Greek" was a familiar phrase for "silly person")

5   *I shall give worse payment*

    I.e., I'll beat you.

6   *thou hast an open hand*

    I.e., you are generous.

7   *after fourteen years' purchase*

    I.e., at a high price. The value of a property was usually twelve times the yearly rent, so the general meaning of the sentence is: "Wise men who give money to fools end up buying themselves good reputations—though they have to pay more than the usual rate to get it."

Act 4, Scene 1

Enter **Sebastian** *and* [**Feste**, *the*] *clown.*

Feste

Will you¹ make me believe that I am not sent for you?

Sebastian

free   Go to, go to, thou art a foolish fellow. Let me be clear°
of thee.

Feste

Well held out,² i' faith. No, I do not know you, nor I am
not sent to you by my lady to bid you come speak with   5
her, nor your name is not Master Cesario, nor this is
not my nose neither. Nothing that is so is so.

Sebastian

express   I prithee, vent° thy folly somewhere else. Thou know'st
not me.

Feste

"Vent" my folly? He has heard that word of some great man   10
and now applies it to a fool. "Vent" my folly! I am afraid this
oaf / affected fop   great lubber,° the world, will prove a cockney.° I prithee
now, ungird thy strangeness³ and tell me what I shall "vent"
to my lady. Shall I "vent "to her that thou art coming?

Sebastian

I prithee, foolish Greek,⁴ depart from me. There's   15
money for thee. [*hands him money*] If you tarry longer, I
shall give worse payment.⁵

Feste

faith   By my troth,° thou hast an open hand.⁶ These wise men
reputation   that give fools money get themselves a good report°—
after fourteen years' purchase.⁷   20

Enter [**Sir**] **Andrew**, [**Sir**] **Toby** [**Belch**], *and* **Fabian**.

1   *have an action of battery against him*

     **Bring a lawsuit against him for
     assault.**

2   *well fleshed*

     **I.e., an experienced fighter (*fleshed*
     meaning "bloodied" or initiated
     into battle)**

Sir Andrew

[*to* **Sebastian**] Now, sir, have I met you again? There's
for you. [*striking* **Sebastian**]

Sebastian

[*beating* **Sir Andrew**] Why, there's for thee, and there,
and there. Are all the people mad?

Sir Toby Belch

Stop   Hold,° sir, or I'll throw your dagger o'er the house.   25

Feste

at once   [*aside*] This will I tell my lady straight.° I would not be in
some of, your coats for two pence.   [*He exits.*]

Sir Toby Belch

[*restraining* **Sebastian**] Come on, sir; hold!

Sir Andrew

Nay, let him alone. I'll go another way to work with
him. I'll have an action of battery against him, [1] if there   30
be any law in Illyria. Though I struck him first, yet it's
no matter for that.

Sebastian

[*to* **Sir Toby Belch**] Let go thy hand!

Sir Toby Belch

Come, sir, I will not let you go. Come, my young soldier,
sword   put up your iron.° You are well fleshed. [2] Come on.   35

Sebastian

I will be free from thee. [*pulls away, drawing his sword*] What
wouldst thou now? If thou dar'st tempt me further,
draw thy sword.

Sir Toby Belch

What, what? Nay, then I must have an ounce or two of
impudent   this malapert° blood from you. [*draws his sword*]   40

1   *botched up*

    Crudely contrived

2   *He started one poor heart of mine in thee.*

    **I.e., (by attacking you) he
    frightened my heart, which is
    within your body (because I have
    given it to you in love). This line
    involves several puns on hunting
    terms: *heart* sounds like "hart," or
    "stag," while to *start* a hunted
    animal is to rouse it from its hiding
    place.**

3   *relish*

    **I.e., meaning; sense (*relish* literally
    means "taste")**

4   *Let fancy still my sense in Lethe steep*

    **I.e., let me always remain in this
    fantasy and forget who I really am.
    Lethe is the river of forgetfulness
    that runs through Hades, the Hell
    of Greek mythology.**

Enter **Olivia**.

Olivia
Hold, Toby! On thy life I charge thee, hold!
Sir Toby Belch
Madam!
Olivia
Will it be ever thus? Ungracious wretch,
Fit for the mountains and the barbarous caves,
Where manners ne'er were preached! Out of my sight!   45
—Be not offended, dear Cesario.

Ruffian   —Rudesby,° be gone!

                    [**Sir Toby Belch**, **Sir Andrew**, *and* **Fabian** *exit.*]
                              I prithee, gentle friend,

influence you   Let thy fair wisdom, not thy passion, sway°
assault   In this uncivil and unjust extent°
                   Against thy peace. Go with me to my house   50
                   And hear thou there how many fruitless pranks
                   This ruffian hath botched up,¹ that thou thereby
                   Mayst smile at this. Thou shalt not choose but go.
refuse / Curse   Do not deny.° Beshrew° his soul for me!
                   He started one poor heart of mine in thee.²   55
Sebastian
                   [*aside*] What relish³ is in this? How runs the stream?
Either   Or° I am mad or else this is a dream.
                   Let fancy still my sense in Lethe steep;⁴
                   If it be thus to dream, still let me sleep!
Olivia
I wish   Nay, come, I prithee. Would° thou'dst be ruled by me!   60
Sebastian
                   Madam, I will.
Olivia
                              Oh, say so, and so be!   *They exit.*

1   *Sir Topas*

    **Topaz, the yellow gemstone, was
    believed to cure lunacy. Geoffrey
    Chaucer's *Canterbury Tales* and John
    Lyly's *Endimion*, two works well
    known to Shakespeare and his
    audience, also feature comic
    characters named Topas, though in
    both they are knights.**

2   *the whilst*

    In the meantime

3   *to become the function well*

    **I.e., to do the job (of priest)
    appropriately**

4   *lean enough to be thought a good
    student*

    **I.e., sufficiently poverty stricken to
    be a credible scholar (of theology)**

5   *housekeeper*

    Innkeeper (i.e., host)

6   *goes as fairly*

    Sounds as good

7   Bonos dies

    **Good day (either an unintentional
    mispronunciation or an
    intentional parody of the Spanish,
    buenos dias)**

8   *old hermit of Prague*

    **Yet another of Feste's invented
    scholarly authorities.**

9   *King Gorboduc*

    A legendary king of early Britain

Act 4, Scene 2

Enter **Maria** *and* [**Feste**, *the*] *Clown.*

is dressed up as a priest to go visit Malvolio in crazy house

Maria

Nay, I prithee, put on this gown and this beard. Make

parish priest him believe thou art Sir Topas[1] the curate.° Do it

quickly. I'll call Sir Toby the whilst.[2]   [*She exits.*]

Feste

disguise   Well, I'll put it on, and I will dissemble° myself in 't;

told lies   and I would I were the first that ever dissembled° in   5

such a gown. [*puts on the gown and beard*] I am not

tall enough to become the function well,[3] nor lean

enough to be thought a good student,[4] but to be

reputed as   said° an honest man and a good housekeeper[5] goes as

fairly[6] as to say a careful man and a great scholar. The   10

colleagues   competitors° enter.

Enter [**Sir**] **Toby** [**Belch** *and* **Maria**].

Sir Toby Belch

Jove bless thee, master Parson.

Feste

Bonos dies,[7] Sir Toby. For, as the old hermit of Prague,[8]

that never saw pen and ink, very wittily said to a niece

of King Gorboduc,[9] "That that is, is," so I, being Master   15

Parson, am Master Parson. For, what is "that" but

"that," and "is" but "is"?

Sir Toby Belch

Go to   To° him, Sir Topas.

Feste

[*disguising his voice*] What ho, I say! Peace in this prison!

1   *Out, hyperbolical fiend!*

    "Leave, ranting devil!" Feste, in his
    role as Sir Topas, addresses the
    devil that has supposedly
    possessed Malvolio.

2   *hideous darkness*

    Enclosing the insane in a dark
    room was a standard treatment in
    early modern England.

3   *transparent as barricadoes*

    As transparent as wooden
    barricades. In this passage, Feste
    speaks in deliberate contradictions
    further to confuse the already
    disoriented Malvolio.

4   *clerestories*

    A row of windows located high on a
    wall (particularly in churches)

5   *ebony*

    A kind of dull, black wood (and
    therefore unlikely to be *lustrous*)

6   *of obstruction*

    I.e., of the light being shut out

Sir Toby Belch

pretends The knave counterfeits° well. A good knave.   20

Malvolio

[*within*] Who calls there?

Feste

Sir Topas the curate, who comes to visit Malvolio the
lunatic.

Malvolio

Sir Topas, Sir Topas, good Sir Topas, go to my lady—

Feste

torment Out, hyperbolical fiend![1] How vexest° thou this man!   25
—Talkest thou nothing but of ladies?

Sir Toby Belch

[*to* **Feste**] Well said, Master Parson.

Malvolio

Sir Topas, never was man thus wronged. Good Sir
Topas, do not think I am mad. They have laid me here
in hideous darkness.[2]   30

Feste

mild Fie, thou dishonest Satan! I call thee by the most modest°
treat terms, for I am one of those gentle ones that will use°
i.e., room the devil himself with courtesy. Say'st thou that house°
is dark?

Malvolio

As Hell, Sir Topas.   35

Feste

Why, it hath bay windows transparent as barricadoes,[3]
and the clerestories[4] toward the south-north are as
lustrous as ebony.[5] And yet complainest thou of
obstruction?[6]

Malvolio

I am not mad, Sir Topas. I say to you this house is dark.   40

1   *Egyptians in their fog*

In Exodus 10:21–23, darkness was one of the ten plagues with which God struck Egypt as Moses attempted to liberate the enslaved Israelites.

2   *Make the trial of it in any constant question.*

Test my sanity with any kind of cogent questioning.

3   *Pythagoras*

Ancient Greek philosopher who believed that souls could transmigrate, that is, successively inhabit the bodies of various kinds of creatures

4   *allow of thy wits*

I.e., attest to your sanity

5   *I am for all waters*

I.e., I can handle anything. The origin of the phrase is obscure, but it probably has the literal meaning "I'm prepared for all kinds of weather."

6   *Thou mightst have done this without thy beard and gown. He sees thee not.*

Maria's speech indicates that in the original staging of this scene Malvolio was not visible to the audience. On an Elizabethan stage this could have meant that the actor was concealed behind a curtain, either in a doorway or in front of a recessed space between the tiring-house doors, which would not muffle his voice unduly (see David Carnegie's entry in the "For Further Reading" section). Some commentators have argued that this line suggests that the scene is in an uneven state of composition; others have argued that it permits Feste a virtuoso turn. First he garbs himself as a priest, which allows him a few jokes about clerics, and then later, without the costume, he is able to reveal that it is not habit but the voice alone that makes the character. Feste demonstrates a similar vocal virtuosity in his song beginning at line 4.2.69, which is a dialogue written for two voices.

Feste

Madman, thou errest. I say, there is no darkness but
befuddled   ignorance, in which thou art more puzzled° than the
Egyptians in their fog. [1]

Malvolio

I say this house is as dark as ignorance, though ignorance were as dark as Hell, and I say there was never   45
man thus abused: I am no more mad than you are.
Make the trial of it in any constant question. [2]

Feste

What is the opinion of Pythagoras [3] concerning wildfowl?

Malvolio

grandmother / perhaps   That the soul of our grandam° might haply° inhabit a
bird.   50

Feste

What think'st thou of his opinion?

Malvolio

agree with   I think nobly of the soul, and no way approve° his
opinion.

Feste

Fare thee well. Remain thou still in darkness. Thou
shalt hold th' opinion of Pythagoras ere I will allow of   55
thy wits, [4] and fear to kill a woodcock lest thou dispos-
sess the soul of thy grandam. Fare thee well.

Malvolio

Sir Topas, Sir Topas!

Sir Toby Belch

[*to* **Feste**] My most exquisite Sir Topas!

Feste

[*in his own voice*] Nay, I am for all waters. [5]   60

Maria

Thou mightst have done this without thy beard and
gown. He sees thee not. [6]

1   *To him in thine own voice*

**Go to him (i.e., Malvolio) and
speak in your normal voice.**

2   *Hey, Robin, jolly Robin, / Tell me how
thy lady does.*

**A traditional folksong about a man
who laments the unfaithfulness of
his lover.**

3   *pardie*

**I.e., by God (an anglicization of the
French *par dieu*)**

Sir Toby Belch

To him in thine own voice[1] and bring me word how
thou find'st him. I would we were well rid of this
set free   knavery. If he may be conveniently delivered,° I would   65
he were, for I am now so far in offense with my niece
that I cannot pursue with any safety this sport to
conclusion   the upshot.° Come by and by to my chamber.

                    [**Sir Toby Belch** *and* **Maria**] *exit.*

Feste

   [*sings*] Hey, Robin, jolly Robin,
   Tell me how thy lady does.[2]   70

Malvolio   → "bad will"

Fool!

Feste

   [*sings*] My lady is unkind, pardie.[3]

Malvolio

Fool!

Feste

   [*sings*] Alas, why is she so?

Malvolio

Fool, I say!   75

Feste

   [*sings*] She loves another—

                         [*speaks*] Who calls, ha?

Malvolio

Good fool, as ever thou wilt deserve well at my hand,
help me to a candle, and pen, ink, and paper. As I am a
gentleman, I will live to be thankful to thee for 't.

Feste

Master Malvolio?   80

Malvolio

Ay, good fool.

1   *how fell you besides your five wits*

    **How did you come to be out of
    your mind?**

2   *But as well?*

    Only that well?

3   *propertied me*

    **Treated me as though I were
    nothing more than a piece of
    property**

Feste

Alas, sir, how fell you besides your five wits?[1]

Malvolio

outrageously Fool, there was never a man so notoriously° abused. I
am as well in my wits, fool, as thou art.

Feste

But as well?[2] Then you are mad indeed, if you be no   85
better in your wits than a fool.

Malvolio

They have here propertied me,[3] keep me in darkness,
send ministers to me—asses!—and do all they can to
harass face° me out of my wits.

Feste

Watch Advise° you what you say. The minister is here. [*disguis-*   90
ing his voice again] Malvolio, Malvolio, thy wits the heav-
ens restore! Endeavor thyself to sleep and leave thy
nonsense talk vain bibble-babble.°

Malvolio

Sir Topas!

Feste

[*as Sir Topas*] Maintain no words with him, good fellow.   95
be with [*in his own voice*] Who, I, sir? Not I, sir. God by° you , good
Sir Topas. [*as Sir Topas*] Marry, amen. [*in his own voice*] I
will, sir, I will.

Malvolio

Fool! Fool! Fool, I say!

Feste

reprimanded Alas, sir, be patient. What say you sir? I am shent° for   100
speaking to you.

Malvolio

Good fool, help me to some light and some paper. I tell
thee, I am as well in my wits as any man in Illyria.

1   *Well-a-day that you were*

I.e., alas, if only you were

2   *Like to the old Vice*

Like the character of the Vice. In
the medieval drama that preceded
Shakespeare, the Vice was a comic
stock character, a predecessor of
the fools and jesters of Elizabethan
comedies.

3   *Who, with dagger of lath, / In his rage
and his wrath, / Cries "Aha," to the devil*

Who, with his dagger made of wood
(i.e., a stage prop, not a genuine
weapon), in anger and fury screams
defiantly at the devil. One of the
comic routines traditionally
associated with the Vice involved
him outwitting and sometimes
physically harming the devil.

4   *Pare thy nails, dad.*

Cut your nails, father. This was
probably a familiar bit of stage
business, as suggested by
Shakespeare's *Henry V*'s reference to
"this roaring devil i 'th' old play, that
everyone may pare his nails with a
wooden dagger" (4.4.69–70).

Feste

Well-a-day that you were, [1] sir.

Malvolio

By this hand, I am. Good fool, some ink, paper, and   105

write   light, and convey what I will set° down to my lady. It

benefit   shall advantage° thee more than ever the bearing of

letter did.

Feste

I will help you to 't. But tell me true, are you not mad

pretend   indeed, or do you but counterfeit?°   110

Malvolio

Believe me, I am not. I tell thee true.

Feste

Nay, I'll ne'er believe a madman till I see his brains. I

will fetch you light and paper and ink.

Malvolio

repay   Fool, I'll requite° it in the highest degree. I prithee, be

gone.   115

Feste

[*sings*] I am gone, sir,

soon   And anon,° sir,

I'll be with you again,

moment   In a trice,°

Like to the old Vice, [2]   120

Your need to sustain,

Who, with dagger of lath,

In his rage and his wrath,

Cries "Aha," to the devil, [3]

Like a mad lad: 125

"Pare thy nails, dad. [4]

master   Adieu, goodman° devil."   *He exits.*

Twelfth Night

1 *my soul disputes well with my sense*
   **My intelligence and my senses
   agree.**

2 *Take and give back affairs and their
   dispatch*
   **Take on important matters and
   deal with them efficiently.**

3 *chantry by*
   Private chapel close by

Act 4, Scene 3

Enter **Sebastian**.

Sebastian

This is the air; that is the glorious sun;

This pearl she gave me—I do feel 't and see 't—

astonishment   And though 'tis wonder° that enwraps me thus,

Yet 'tis not madness. Where's Antonio, then?

I could not find him at the Elephant.   5

had been / report   Yet there he was,° and there I found this credit°

roam   That he did range° the town to seek me out.

excellent   His counsel now might do me golden° service,

For though my soul disputes well with my sense [1]

That this may be some error, but no madness,   10

unexpected event   Yet doth this accident° and flood of fortune

example   So far exceed all instance,° all discourse,

That I am ready to distrust mine eyes

And wrangle with my reason that persuades me

belief   To any other trust° but that I am mad—   15

Or else the lady's mad. Yet if 'twere so,

rule   She could not sway° her house, command her followers,

Take and give back affairs and their dispatch [2]

With such a smooth, discreet, and stable bearing

As I perceive she does. There's something in 't   20

deceptive   That is deceivable.° But here the lady comes.

Enter **Olivia** *and* **Priest**.

Olivia

[*to* **Sebastian**] Blame not this haste of mine. If you
    mean well,

Now go with me and with this holy man

Into the chantry by. [3] There, before him,

1   *Plight me the full assurance of your faith*
    **Guarantee to me that you'll be
    faithful (i.e., by pledging to
    become my husband; such a
    betrothal was as legally binding as
    a marriage ceremony).**

2   *According to my birth*
    **As befits someone of my social
    status**

And underneath that consecrated roof,   25
Plight me the full assurance of your faith, [1]

anxious / suspicous   That my most jealous° and too doubtful° soul

i.e., The priest   May live at peace. He° shall conceal it

Until / public notice   Whiles° you are willing it shall come to note,°

At which   What° time we will our celebration keep   30
According to my birth. [2] What do you say?

Sebastian

I'll follow this good man and go with you,
And, having sworn truth, ever will be true.

Olivia

Then lead the way, good Father, and heavens so shine

favorably   That they may fairly° note this act of mine.   *They exit.*   35

1   *This is to give a dog and in recompense*
    desire my dog again.

    Very likely a reference to an
    anecdote circulating about Queen
    Elizabeth. One of the Queen's
    kinsmen had a dog he loved very
    much; the Queen asked him to give
    her the pet, for which she would
    grant him a favor in return. The
    kinsman agreed, and when it came
    time to ask for his favor, he
    requested his dog back.

Act 5, Scene 1

*Enter [**Feste**, *the*] *Clown and* **Fabian**.*

Fabian

Now, as thou lov'st me, let me see his° letter.

i.e., Malvolio's

Feste

Good Master Fabian, grant me another request.

Fabian

Anything.

Feste

Do not desire to see this letter.

Fabian

This is to give a dog and in recompense desire my dog   5
again. ¹

*Enter Duke [**Orsino**], **Viola**, **Curio**, *and lords.**

Orsino

Belong you to the Lady Olivia, friends?

Feste

Ay, sir, we are some of her trappings.°

ornaments

Orsino

I know thee well. How dost thou, my good fellow?

Feste

Truly, sir, the better for my foes and the worse for my   10
friends.

Orsino

Just the contrary: the better for thy friends.

Feste

No, sir, the worse.

Orsino

How can that be?

1 *conclusions to be as kisses, if your four negatives make your two affirmatives*

Grammatically, four negatives may make *two affirmatives*, since a "double negative" makes a positive statement. Perhaps Feste is merely pointing to how expectations may be surprisingly reversed or more specifically to a familiar literary trope, as in Philip Sidney's *Astrophel and Stella* (Sonnet 63) in which a man attempts to kiss a lady. The woman says "no" twice, which the man perversely interprets as permission to kiss her.

2 *double-dealing*

(1) hypocrisy, double-crossing; (2) giving (money) twice

3 *put your grace in your pocket*

(1) put aside your virtue (which might prevent you from listening to such *ill counsel*; (2) put your own hand (*your Grace* is a customary address to a duke) in your pocket (where your money is).

4 *let your flesh and blood obey it*

I.e., let your human instincts follow my *ill counsel* (as opposed to your *grace*).

5 *Primo, secundo, tertio is a good play*

I.e., one, two, three is a good game. This alludes, perhaps, to a child's game (or *play*) that begins with a player calling out, "one, two, three!" Throughout this passage, Feste is attempting to wheedle a third coin out of Orsino.

6 *the third pays for all*

I.e., the third time's the charm

7 *triplex*

In music, a triple-time beat

8 *Saint Bennet*

I.e., Saint Benedict's Church (which was the name of a church across the river from the Globe Theatre)

Feste

Marry, sir, they praise me and make an ass of me. Now   15
my foes tell me plainly I am an ass, so that by my foes,
sir, I profit in the knowledge of myself, and by my

deceived   friends I am abused;° so that, conclusions to be as
kisses, if your four negatives make your two
affirmatives, [1] why then the worse for my friends and   20
the better for my foes.

Orsino

Why, this is excellent.

Feste

even though   By my troth, sir, no—though° it please you to be one of
my friends.

Orsino

[*gives a coin*] Thou shalt not be the worse for me: there's   25
gold.

Feste

If it were not   But° that it would be double-dealing, [2] sir, I would you
could make it another.

Orsino

Oh, you give me ill counsel.

Feste

Put your grace in your pocket, [3] sir, for this once, and   30
let your flesh and blood obey it. [4]

Orsino

i.e., as to   Well, I will be so much a sinner to° be a double-dealer;
there's another. [*gives him another coin*]

Feste

Primo, secundo, tertio is a good play, [5] and, the old saying
is, the third pays for all. [6] The triplex, [7] sir, is a good   35
lively   tripping° measure, or the bells of Saint Bennet, [8] sir,
may put you in mind—one, two, three.

1   *throw*

Throw of the dice (i.e., this play)

2   *Vulcan*

The blacksmith of the Roman
gods, often depicted as blackened
by smoke and soot.

3   *For shallow draft and bulk unprizable*

Not very valuable, due to its small
size and its lightness (*draft* being
the amount of water displaced by a
ship).

4   *scatheful grapple*

Destructive battle

5   *That very envy and the tongue of loss /
Cried fame and honor on him*

That even the animosity (of his
enemies) and the voices of those
who were defeated said he should
be honored (for his valor).

6   Phoenix

Name of a ship in Orsino's navy.

7   *Candy*

I.e., Candia, a city in Crete.

8   Tiger

Another ship in Orsino's navy.

9   *desperate of shame and state*

Recklessly disregarding his
reputation and his situation.

Orsino

You can fool no more money out of me at this throw.[1]
If you will let your lady know I am here to speak with
her and bring her along with you, it may awake my   40
generosity   bounty° further.

Feste

Marry, sir, lullaby to your bounty till I come again. I go,
sir, but I would not have you to think that my desire of
having is the sin of covetousness. But, as you say, sir,
let your bounty take a nap; I will awake it anon. *He exits.* 45

                    Enter **Antonio** *and* **Officers**.

Viola

Here comes the man, sir, that did rescue me.

Orsino

That face of his I do remember well,
Yet when I saw it last it was besmeared
As black as Vulcan[2] in the smoke of war.
contemptible   A baubling° vessel was he captain of,   50
For shallow draft and bulk unprizable,[3]
With which such scatheful grapple[4] did he make
ship   With the most noble bottom° of our fleet,
That very envy and the tongue of loss
Cried fame and honor on him.[5]—What's the matter?   55

First Officer

Orsino, this is that Antonio
That took the *Phoenix*[6] and her freight from Candy,[7]
And this is he that did the *Tiger*[8] board
When your young nephew Titus lost his leg.
Here in the streets, desperate of shame and state,[9]   60
brawl   In private brabble° did we apprehend him.

1   *drew on my side*

    **Drew his sword and fought on my
    behalf**

2   *put strange speech upon me*

    Said strange things to me

3   *but distraction*

    I.e., if not insanity

4   *brought thee to their mercies*

    **Brought you into the hands of
    those**

5   *on base and ground enough*

    With solid justification

6   *All his in dedication*

    **I.e., (my love was) dedicated
    entirely to him**

7   *to face me out of his acquaintance*

    **I.e., to deny to my face that he
    knew me**

8   *And grew a twenty-years-removèd thing /
    While one would wink*

    **Made himself like someone who
    hasn't seen me in twenty years, in
    the amount of time it takes to blink
    one's eyes**

Viola

He did me kindness, sir, drew on my side, [1]

But in conclusion put strange speech upon me. [2]

I know not what 'twas but distraction. [3]

Orsino

Infamous   Notable° pirate! Thou saltwater thief,   65

What foolish boldness brought thee to their mercies [4]

grievous   Whom thou, in terms so bloody and so dear,°

Hast made thine enemies?

Antonio

                    Orsino, noble sir,

Be pleased that I shake off these names you give me.

Antonio never yet was thief or pirate,   70

Though, I confess, on base and ground enough, [5]

Orsino's enemy. A witchcraft drew me hither.

That most ingrateful boy there by your side

From the rude sea's enraged and foamy mouth

rescue   Did I redeem.° A wreck past hope he was.   75

His life I gave him and did thereto add

reservation   My love, without retention° or restraint,

All his in dedication. [6] For his sake

simply   Did I expose myself, pure° for his love,

hostile   Into the danger of this adverse° town,   80

attacked   Drew to defend him when he was beset,°

Where, being apprehended, his false cunning,

intending   (Not meaning° to partake with me in danger)

Taught him to face me out of his acquaintance [7]

And grew a twenty-years-removèd thing   85

While one would wink, [8] denied me mine own purse,

committed   Which I had recommended° to his use

Not half an hour before.

Viola

How can this be?

1   *What would my lord, but that he may*
    not have

    **What does my lord want, other
    than what he can't have (i.e., my
    love).**

2   *keep promise with me*

    **Honor the promise you made me
    (see 4.3.33).**

3   *Good my lord*

    **Olivia asks Orsino to let Cesario
    speak.**

4   *fat and fulsome*

    I.e., gross and repulsive

Orsino

[*to* **Antonio**] When came he to this town?   *90*

Antonio

Today, my lord, and for three months before,

interruption / interval   No interim,° not a minute's vacancy,°

Both day and night did we keep company.

Enter **Olivia** *and attendants.*

Orsino

Here comes the Countess. Now Heaven walks on Earth.

as for   But for° thee, fellow— fellow, thy words are madness: *95*

Three months this youth hath tended upon me.

But more of that anon. [*to an officer*] Take him aside.

Olivia

What would my lord, but that he may not have,[1]

of use   Wherein Olivia may seem serviceable?°

Cesario, you do not keep promise with me.[2]   *100*

Viola

Madam?

Orsino

Gracious Olivia—

Olivia

What do you say, Cesario?——Good my lord[3]—

Viola

My lord would speak. My duty hushes me.

Olivia

anything   If it be aught° to the old tune, my lord,   *105*

It is as fat and fulsome[4] to mine ear

As howling after music.

Orsino

                Still so cruel?

1 *Like to th' Egyptian thief at point of death, / Kill what I love*

In **Ethiopica**, a romance by the ancient Greek writer Heliodorus, an Egyptian criminal on the verge of being killed tries to murder his lover in order to keep her from his captors.

2 *savors nobly*

Suggests nobility

3 *to nonregardance cast my faith*

Treat my love with complete disregard

4 *Live you*

Carry on living

5 *that cruel eye*

I.e., Olivia's eye, which regards Cesario with love

6 *in his master's spite*

Against the best interests of his master

7 *a raven's heart within a dove*

I.e., the cruel heart inside Olivia's beautiful body

8 *do you rest*

Put your mind at ease

Olivia

Still so constant, lord.

Orsino

What, to perverseness? You uncivil lady,

ungrateful / inauspicious To whose ingrate° and unauspicious° altars   110

My soul the faithful'st off'rings have breathed out

offered That e'er devotion tendered.° What shall I do?

Olivia

Exactly / suit Even° what it please my lord that shall become° him.

Orsino

Why should I not, had I the heart to do it,

Like to th' Egyptian thief at point of death,   115

Kill what I love? [1]—a savage jealousy

That sometimes savors nobly. [2] But hear me this:

Since you to nonregardance cast my faith, [3]

since And that° I partly know the instrument

wrenches That screws° me from my true place in your favor,   120

Live you [4] the marble-breasted tyrant still;

darling But this your minion,° whom I know you love,

regard And whom, by Heaven I swear, I tender° dearly,

Him will I tear out of that cruel eye [5]

Where he sits crownèd in his master's spite. [6]   125

with —Come, boy, with me. My thoughts are ripe in° mischief.

I'll sacrifice the lamb that I do love

To spite a raven's heart within a dove. [7] [*starts to leave*]

Viola

happily / ready And I, most jocund,° apt,° and willingly,

To do you rest, [8] a thousand deaths would die.   130

[*follows* **Orsino**]

Olivia

Where goes Cesario?

Viola

After him I love

1   *by all mores*
    By all such comparisons

2   *you witnesses above*
    I.e., the gods in Heaven

3   *sirrah*
    **A form of address normally used
    for social inferiors; sometimes, as
    here, it is expressive of mild
    derision.**

4   *That makes thee strangle thy propriety*
    **That motivates you to deny your
    identity (as my husband)**

5   *Take thy fortunes up.*
    Embrace your destiny.

More than I love these eyes, more than my life,
More, by all mores,¹ than e'er I shall love wife.
If I do feign, you witnesses above²

the corruption Punish my life for tainting° of my love! 135

Olivia

deceived Ay me, detested! How am I beguiled!°

Viola

Who does beguile you? Who does do you wrong?

Olivia

Hast thou forgot thyself? Is it so long?
—Call forth the holy Father. [*An attendant exits.*]

Orsino

[*to* **Viola**] Come, away!

Olivia

Whither, my lord?—Cesario, husband, stay. 140

Orsino

Husband?

Olivia

Ay, husband. Can he that deny?

Orsino

Her husband, sirrah?³

Viola

No, my lord, not I.

Olivia

ignobleness Alas, it is the baseness° of thy fear
That makes thee strangle thy propriety.⁴
Fear not, Cesario. Take thy fortunes up.⁵ 145

that which Be that° thou know'st thou art, and then thou art

that which (i.e., Orsino) As great as that° thou fear'st.

Enter **Priest**.

1   *Sealed in my function*

    **Authorized by me in my capacity
    (as priest)**

2   *hath sowed a grizzle on thy case*

    **Has put a gray beard on your face
    (i.e., when you grow into maturity)**

3   *That thine own trip shall be thine over-
    throw*

    **I.e., that the deceit you practice
    against others will be your own
    undoing (a *trip* being a wrestling
    move in which one fighter trips up
    his opponent)**

Oh, welcome, Father!

Father, I charge thee by thy reverence

reveal   Here to unfold° (though lately we intended

circumstance   To keep in darkness what occasion° now   150

Reveals before 'tis ripe) what thou dost know

recently   Hath newly° passed between this youth and me.

Priest

A contract of eternal bond of love,

joining   Confirmed by mutual joinder° of your hands,

union   Attested by the holy close° of lips,   155

exchange   Strengthened by interchangement° of your rings,

contract   And all the ceremony of this compact°

Sealed in my function [1] by my testimony,

Since when, my watch hath told me, toward my grave

I have traveled but two hours.   160

Orsino

lying   [*to* **Viola**] O thou dissembling° cub! What wilt thou be

When time hath sowed a grizzle on thy case? [2]

craftiness   Or will not else thy craft° so quickly grow

That thine own trip shall be thine overthrow? [3]

Farewell and take her, but direct thy feet   165

Where thou and I henceforth may never meet.

Viola

My lord, I do protest—

Olivia

Oh, do not swear!

Keep a   Hold° little faith, though thou hast too much fear.

Enter **Sir Andrew**.

Sir Andrew

immediately   For the love of God, a surgeon! Send one presently° to

Sir Toby!   170

1 *broke my head across*

   Split my head open

2 *coxcomb*

   **I.e., head. Fool's caps were
   sometimes called *coxcombs*, for
   their resemblance to the flaps of
   skin (*comb*) on a cock's head.**

3 *incardinate*

   **A (perhaps drunken)
   mispronunciation of *incarnate*,
   meaning "in the flesh."**

4 *'Od's lifelings*

   **A mild oath: by God's little lives
   (usually "by God's life")**

5 *bespake you fair*

   Spoke to you with courtesy

6 *set nothing by*

   Think nothing of

Olivia

What's the matter?

Sir Andrew

He has   H' as° broke my head across¹ and has given Sir Toby a

bloody coxcomb² too. For the love of God, your help! I

had rather than forty pound I were at home.

Olivia

Who has done this, Sir Andrew?   175

Sir Andrew

The Count's gentleman, one Cesario. We took him for a

coward, but he's the very devil incardinate.³

Orsino

My gentleman, Cesario?

Sir Andrew

'Od's lifelings,⁴ here he is!—You broke my head for

no reason   nothing,° and that that I did, I was set on to do 't by Sir   180

Toby.

Viola

Why do you speak to me? I never hurt you.

You drew your sword upon me without cause,

But I bespake you fair⁵ and hurt you not.

Sir Andrew

If a bloody coxcomb be a hurt, you have hurt me. I   185

think you set nothing by⁶ a bloody coxcomb.

*Enter [**Sir**] **Toby** [**Belch**] and [**Feste**, the] Clown.*

limping   Here comes Sir Toby halting.° You shall hear more. But

beat   if he had not been in drink, he would have tickled°

in other ways   you othergates° than he did.

Orsino

How now, gentleman? How is 't with you?   190

1   *That's all one*

    It doesn't matter.

2   *a passy-measures pavin*

    A slow mover. Toby drunkenly
    anglicizes the Italian *passamezzo
    pavana*, a stately dance set to slow
    music.

3   *we'll be dressed*

    I.e., our wounds will be cleaned
    and bandaged

4   *the brother of my blood*

    My own biological brother

5   *with wit and safety*

    I.e., with reasonable care for my
    own well-being

6   *throw a strange regard upon me*

    Look at me strangely

Sir Toby Belch
That's all one: [1] h' as° hurt me, and there's the end on 't. *(he has)*
[*to* **Feste**] Sot,° didst see Dick Surgeon, sot? *(Drunkard)*

Feste
Oh, he's drunk, Sir Toby—an hour agone.° His eyes were *(ago)*
set° at eight i' th' morning. *(closed)*

Sir Toby Belch
Then he's a rogue, and a passy-measures pavin. [2] I hate 195
a drunken rogue.

Olivia
Away with him! Who hath made this havoc with them?

Sir Andrew
I'll help you, Sir Toby, because we'll be dressed [3]
together.

Sir Toby Belch
Will you help? An ass-head, and a coxcomb,° and a 200 *(i.e., fool)*
knave, a thin-faced knave, a gull!° *(patsy)*

Olivia
Get him to bed and let his hurt be looked to.
[**Sir Toby Belch**, **Sir Andrew**, **Fabian**, *and* **Feste** *exit.*]

Enter **Sebastian**. → reveal

Sebastian
I am sorry, madam, I have hurt your kinsman,
But, had it been the brother of my blood, [4]
I must have done no less with wit and safety. [5] 205
You throw a strange regard upon me, [6] and by that
I do perceive it hath offended you.
Pardon me, sweet one, even for the vows
We made each other but so late° ago. *(recently)*

Orsino
One face, one voice, one habit,° and two persons! 210 *(suit of clothes)*

1   *A natural perspective*

**An optical illusion created by
nature. A *perspective* was a
Renaissance apparatus that
distorted images, or a trick
painting, here imagined as turning
a single figure into two.**

2   *racked*

**I.e., put me on the rack. A rack was
a wooden-framed torture device
on which victims were painfully
stretched.**

3   *Fear'st thou that*

I.e., do you doubt that

4   *Nor can there be that deity in my nature /
Of here and everywhere*

**Nor do I possess that divine ability
to be everywhere at once**

5   *Of charity*

**(Tell me) out of the goodness of
your heart**

6   *But am in that dimension grossly clad /
Which from the womb I did participate*

**But I am still dressed in the same
mortal body I've had since birth.**

7   *as the rest goes even*

As everything seems to suggest

A natural perspective,[1] that is and is not!

Sebastian

Antonio, O my dear Antonio!

How have the hours racked[2] and tortured me

Since I have lost thee!

Antonio

Sebastian are you?

Sebastian

      Fear'st thou that,[3] Antonio?   215

Antonio

How have you made division of yourself?

alike An apple, cleft in two, is not more twin°

Than these two creatures. Which is Sebastian?

Olivia

astonishing Most wonderful!°

Sebastian

[*staring at* **Viola**] Do I stand there? I never had a brother,   220

Nor can there be that deity in my nature

Of here and everywhere.[4] I had a sister,

Whom the blind waves and surges have devoured.

Of charity,[5] what kin are you to me?

What countryman? What name? What parentage?   225

Viola

Of Messaline. Sebastian was my father;

Such a Sebastian was my brother too,

dressed So went he suited° to his watery tomb.

clothing If spirits can assume both form and suit°

You come to fright us.

Sebastian

      A spirit I am indeed,   230

But am in that dimension grossly clad

Which from the womb I did participate.[6]

Were you a woman, as the rest goes even,[7]

1   *My father had a mole upon his brow*

     (See LONGER NOTE, page 289.)

2   *maiden weeds*

     Woman's clothes

3   *But nature to her bias drew in that*

     **The metaphor is drawn from a game of
     bowls, in which a weight placed within
     a ball causes the ball to swerve in its
     path. (See LONGER NOTE, page 289.)**

4   *maid and man*

     **I.e., a man who is still a virgin.
     Sebastian may also be suggesting
     that, since he and Viola are so similar
     (and since she fell in love first with
     Cesario), Olivia has essentially found
     herself *betrothed* to both siblings.**

I should my tears let fall upon your cheek
And say "Thrice-welcome, drownèd Viola!"   235

Viola

My father had a mole upon his brow [1]—

Sebastian

And so had mine.

Viola

And died that day when Viola from her birth
Had numbered thirteen years.

Sebastian

memory / still living   Oh, that record° is lively° in my soul!   240
He finishèd indeed his mortal act
That day that made my sister thirteen years.

Viola

hinders   If nothing lets° to make us happy both
But this my masculine usurped attire,
Do not embrace me till each circumstance   245
agree   Of place, time, fortune, do cohere and jump°
That I am Viola—which to confirm,
I'll bring you to a captain in this town,
Where lie my maiden weeds, [2] by whose gentle help
I was preserved to serve this noble Count.   250
All the occurrence of my fortune since
Hath been between this lady and this lord.

Sebastian

[to **Olivia**] So comes it, lady, you have been mistook,
But nature to her bias drew in that. [3]
married   You would have been contracted° to a maid;   255
Nor are you therein, by my life, deceived:
You are betrothed both to a maid and man. [4]

Orsino

[to **Olivia**] Be not amazed. Right noble is his blood.
to reflect truly   If this be so, as yet the glass seems true,°

1   *like to*

    As well as you have loved me

2   *orbèd continent the fire*

    **I.e., the sun. (Literally "spherical
    container of fire")**

3   *upon some action*

    Owing to some legal problem

4   *extracting frenzy*

    **Preoccupying madness (i.e., my
    infatuation with Cesario)**

5   *he holds Beelzebub at the stave's end*

    **I.e., he keeps the devil at some
    distance (*stave's end* = point of a
    lance).**

I shall have share in this most happy wreck.   260
[*to* **Viola**] Boy, thou hast said to me a thousand times
Thou never shouldst love woman like to[1] me.
Viola
swear again and again   And all those sayings will I overswear,°
And those swearings keep as true in soul
As doth that orbèd continent the fire[2]   265
That severs day from night.
Orsino
                                        Give me thy hand
And let me see thee in thy woman's weeds.
Viola
The captain that did bring me first on shore
Hath my maid's garments. He, upon some action,[3]
prison   Is now in durance° at Malvolio's suit,   270
A gentleman and follower of my lady's.
Olivia
free   He shall enlarge° him. Fetch Malvolio hither:
And yet, alas, now I remember me,
insane   They say, poor gentleman, he's much distract.°

Enter [**Feste**, *the*] *Clown with a letter, and* **Fabian**.

A most extracting frenzy[4] of mine own   275
i.e., Malvolio's frenzy   From my remembrance clearly banished his.°
[*to* **Feste**] How does he, sirrah?
Feste
Truly, madam, he holds Beelzebub at the stave's end[5] as
He has   well as a man in his case may do. H' as° here writ a letter
this   to you. I should have given 't you today° morning, but   280
letters / matters   as a madman's epistles° are no gospels, so it skills° not
much when they are delivered.

1 *delivers*

I.e., reads aloud material written
by (but also meaning "sets free")

2 *allow* vox

I.e., permit me to use the
appropriate voice. Feste has begun
reading Malvolio's letter in the *vox*
("voice," in Latin) of a madman.

3 *his right wits*

Malvolio's actual state of mind

4 *thus*

Like this (i.e., in the "mad" voice
I'm trying to use)

5 *as well as your Ladyship*

Just as your Ladyship has the
benefit of her senses

6 *I leave my duty a little unthought of and
speak out of my injury.*

I disregard my proper manners as
your servant and instead speak as
one wronged.

Olivia

Open 't and read it.

Feste

Look then to be well edified when the fool delivers[1] the
madman. [*reads*] "By the Lord, madam,"—   285

Olivia

How now? Art thou mad?

Feste

If   No, madam, I do but read madness. An° your Ladyship
will have it as it ought to be, you must allow *vox*.[2]

Olivia

Prithee, read i' thy right wits.

Feste

So I do, madonna, but to read his right wits[3] is to read   290
consider   thus.[4] Therefore perpend,° my princess, and give ear.

Olivia

[*giving the letter to* **Fabian**] Read it you, sirrah.

Fabian   ⅄ sic

[*reads*] "By the Lord, madam, you wrong me, and the
world shall know it. Though you have put me into darkness and given your drunken cousin rule over me, yet   295
have I the benefit of my senses as well as your Ladyship.[5]
I have your own letter that induced me to the sem-
blance I put on, with the which I doubt not but to do
myself much right or you much shame. Think of me as
you please. I leave my duty a little unthought of and   300
speak out of my injury.[6] The madly used Malvolio."

Olivia

Did he write this?

Feste

Ay, madam.

Orsino

insanity   This savors not much of distraction.°

1   *think me as well a sister as a wife*

**Think as well of me in this new role
as your sister (-in-law) as you would
have thought of me as your wife**

2   *One day shall crown th' alliance on 't*

**At the same time we will sanctify
this new relationship (with a
double wedding)**

Olivia

set free See him delivered,° Fabian; bring him hither.   305

[**Fabian** *exits.*]

[*to* **Orsino**] My lord, so please you, these things further
thought on,

To think me as well a sister as a wife,¹

One day shall crown th' alliance on 't,² so please you,

own Here at my house and at my proper° cost.

Orsino

ready Madam, I am most apt° t' embrace your offer.   310

releases [*to* **Viola**] Your master quits° you, and, for your service done
him

inclination So much against the mettle° of your sex,

upbringing So far beneath your soft and tender breeding,°

And since you called me "master" for so long,

Here is my hand. You shall from this time be   315

Your master's mistress.

Olivia

[*to* **Viola**] A sister! You are she.

Enter [**Fabian**, *with*] **Malvolio**.

Orsino

Is this the madman?

Olivia

Ay, my lord, this same.

—How now, Malvolio!

Malvolio

Madam, you have done me wrong,

Notorious wrong.

Olivia

Have I, Malvolio? No.

1 *in the modesty of honor*

   I.e., as honor would require

2 *acting this*

   Acting according to your instructions

3 *the character*

   The style of my handwriting

4 *And in such forms which here were presupposed / Upon thee*

   And in exactly the manner that was prescribed for you

5 *shrewdly passed*

   Maliciously worked

Malvolio

[hands her a paper] Lady, you have. Pray you, peruse that
    letter.   320

You must not now deny it is your hand.°   *handwriting*

Write from° it if you can, in hand or phrase,   *differently from*

Or say 'tis not your seal, not your invention.°   *composition*

You can say none of this. Well, grant it then,

And tell me, in the modesty of honor,[1]   325

Why you have given me such clear lights° of favor, *i.e., indications*

Bade me come smiling and cross-gartered to you,

To put on yellow stockings, and to frown

Upon Sir Toby and the lighter° people?   *lesser*

And, acting this[2] in an obedient hope,   330

Why have you suffered° me to be imprisoned, *permitted*

Kept in a dark house, visited by the priest,

And made the most notorious geck° and gull° *dupe / fool*

That e'er invention° played on? Tell me why. *trickery*

Olivia

Alas, Malvolio, this is not my writing,   335

Though, I confess, much like the character;[3]

But out of question, 'tis Maria's hand.

And now I do bethink me, it was she

First told me thou wast mad, then cam'st° in smiling, *you came*

And in such forms which here were presupposed   340

Upon thee[4] in the letter. Prithee, be content.

This practice° hath most shrewdly passed[5] upon thee; *plot*

But when we know the grounds and authors° of it, *inventors*

Thou shalt be both the plaintiff and the judge

Of thine own cause.

Fabian

        Good madam, hear me speak,   345

And let no quarrel nor no brawl to come

Taint the condition of this present hour,

1   *Upon some stubborn and uncourteous
    parts / We had conceived against him*

    **Because of some insulting and ill-
    mannered characteristics of his
    that we resented**

2   *whirligig*

    Child's spinning top

Which I have wondered at. In hope it shall not,
Most freely I confess: myself and Toby
Set this device against Malvolio here,   350
Upon some stubborn and uncourteous parts
We had conceived against him.[1] Maria writ

urging   The letter at Sir Toby's great importance,°
In recompense whereof he hath married her.

perpetrated How with a sportful malice it was followed°   355
bring   May rather pluck° on laughter than revenge,
If that the injuries be justly weighed
That have on both sides passed.

Olivia

shamed; undone [*to* **Malvolio**] Alas, poor fool, how have they baffled° thee!

Feste

Why, [*imitating* **Malvolio**] "some are born great, some   360
achieve greatness, and some have greatness thrown
drama   upon them." I was one, sir, in this interlude,° one Sir
Topas, sir, but that's all one. "By the Lord, fool, I am
not mad."—But do you remember? "Madam, why
dull / if laugh you at such a barren° rascal; an° you smile not,   365
he's gagged?" And thus the whirligig[2] of time brings in
his revenges.

Malvolio

I'll be revenged on the whole pack of you.   [*He exits.*]

Olivia

He hath been most notoriously abused.

Orsino

Pursue him and entreat him to a peace.   ⊃ he's a man   370

[*Some attendants exit.*]

He hath not told us of the captain yet.
is convenient When that is known and golden time convents,°
A solemn combination shall be made

1 *so you shall be*

I.e., known as Cesario

2 *mistress*

(1) wife; (2) superior

3 *A foolish thing was but a toy*

I.e., all the foolish things I did were indulged

4 *came to man's estate*

Came of age as a man (*estate* meaning "state" or "condition")

5 *my beds*

I.e., the infirmity of old age

6 *that's all one*

It doesn't matter.

Of our dear souls.—Meantime, sweet sister,

We will not part from hence. —Cesario, come,   375

For so you shall be¹ while you are a man,

But when in other habits you are seen,

love's   Orsino's mistress² and his fancy's° queen.

                                            *They exit, [except for **Feste**].*

Feste

[*sings*] When that I was and a little tiny boy,

With hey, ho, the wind and the rain,   380

A foolish thing was but a toy,³

For the rain it raineth every day.

But when I came to man's estate,⁴

With hey, ho, the wind and the rain,

'Gainst knaves and thieves men shut their gate,   385

For the rain it raineth every day.

But when I came, alas, to wive,

With hey, ho, the wind and the rain,

behaving boorishly   By swaggering° could I never thrive,

For the rain it raineth every day.   390

But when I came unto my beds,⁵

With hey, ho, the wind and the rain,

drunkards / I had   With toss-pots° still had° drunken heads,

For the rain it raineth every day.

A great while ago the world begun,   395

With hey, ho, the wind and the rain,

But that's all one,⁶ our play is done,

And we'll strive to please you every day.   [*He exits.*]

Appendix:
The Songs of *Twelfth Night*
by Claire McEachern

A s befits a play of feasting, *Twelfth Night* is a play saturated with music in several keys. Ross Duffin, in *Shakespeare's Songbook*, lists references to fifteen songs in the play, some original to Shakespeare, and scholars have unearthed contemporary settings for many them, giving us a partial sense of how these songs may have contributed to the play's overall effect. (See Peter Seng's and Ross Duffin's entries in the "Further Reading" section.) In 2.3, Feste offers Sir Toby and Sir Andrew a choice between "a love song or a song of good life," (line 34), and the play's songs generally fall into these two categories: the one melancholic, the other (relatively) rollicking. *Twelfth Night*'s songs may also be categorized, as in Orsino's classifications, as traditional folk songs—"old and plain"—or as contemporary popular music—"light airs and recollected terms / Of these most brisk and giddy-pacèd times" (2.4.5–6)—the latter being what Malvolio, in a snobbish phrase, terms "coziers' catches."

The music of Orsino's household, the "food of love" (1.1.1) tends toward the mournful, even elegiac, "dying fall" (1.1.4) of the love-lament. Most Renaissance love songs seem unable to shake the awareness, either in tone or lyric, that sex is really about death, or as Feste puts it in "O mistress mine," that "Youth's a stuff will not endure." Orsino seems to exhibit a kind of love-hate relationship with music: he both craves it and tires of it quickly, using it to "relieve [his] passion" almost as a kind of catharsis or purge. Sir Toby, however, is Feste's other chief patron, and his tastes run more toward the boisterous drinking songs, rounds, and catches whose performance would be both enhanced and rendered more challenging by the inebriation of their singers. 2.3 begins decorously enough, with a love song for a single voice, but rapidly shakes off this somber moment with a rapid transit into songs of "good life": catches, rounds, snatches of ballads, and onward to a general raucousness and cacophony. The scene then ends, in "Farewell, dear heart," with a parodic rendering of a love song.

The love songs of *Twelfth Night* include the unspecified opening music of 1.1, at Orsino's court; "O mistress mine" (2.3); "Farewell, dear heart" (2.3.95); "Come away, come away, death" (2.4.50); and "Hey, Robin" (sung by Feste outside the dark house of Malvolio). The "light airs" include the two rounds "Hold thy peace" and "Three merry men," as well as a song commemorating a battle ("O' the twelfth day of December"). Sir Toby also refers to "Peg-a-Ramsey," a song about a girl with hair the yellow of Malvolio's stockings, and, somewhat anomalously for his tastes, a song celebrating the constancy of the biblical matron Susannah ("There dwelt a man in Babylon, lady, lady"). Feste's "I am gone, sir," which he sings while parting from the imprisoned Malvolio in 4.2, is an energetic ballad sung in the voice of the devil—appropriate enough, considering that Feste has been undertaking a kind of exorcism. Malvolio's only attempt at song comes in 3.4, "Please one, and please all," a ballad celebrating the capriciousness of female taste; it perhaps unwittingly comments on his own tendency to be, in Maria's phrase, a "time-pleaser" (2.3.136). The closing song of the play, Feste's notorious "When that I was and a little tiny boy," seems original to Shakespeare (it is also alluded to in *King Lear*). In Duffin's conjectured setting, its tone falls somewhere between the elegiac and the rueful. In an Elizabethan staging, the play's close was usually followed by a jig performed by the clown, which was a musical sketch with song and dance. Even as Feste travels between two households, he can sing "both high and low," with a song fit for every occasion and appetite.

Longer Notes

1.2.52   *Thou shalt present me as an eunuch to him.*

Eunuchs, like the mute that the Captain proposes for his own disguise, were associated with the exotic and allegedly barbarous aesthetic of the Turkish court. Viola seems to discard this disguise later in favor of posing as a male page: for instance, in 2.4, Orsino counsels Cesario about his own romantic prospects, prospects that would presumably not exist for a eunuch. This lapse has fueled speculations about Shakespeare's compositional inconsistencies: perhaps he changed his mind about this as he wrote the play, but then forgot to go back and revise this earlier scene. However, other critics have found the image of the eunuch a persistently resonant one in the play: it can signify Viola's loss of her brother, her later description of her own erotic self-sacrifice (2.4.104–117), or serve as a metaphor for the willing renunciation of social status entailed in her disguising her better-born self as a mere page. The abdication of rank involves renouncing what is probably the strongest source of masculine power in the play, a fact underscored by Malvolio's speech in 2.5, in which Malvolio describes the various routes to social "greatness." The speech itself is a paraphrase of Matthew 19.12: "there are some eunuchs, which were so born of their mother's belly: and there be some eunuchs, which be gelded by men, and there be some eunuchs, which have gelded themselves for the kingdom of heaven." The figure of the eunuch was central in the classical comedies of Terence that served as one of Shakespeare's models, and these comedies were themselves based on ancient fertility rites connected with castration rituals. For more, see Keir Elam's and John Astington's entries in the "For Further Reading" section.

Page 107
2.1.36   *so near the manners of my
mother*

Sebastian specifically identifies his
mother with this "female" proclivity
to weeping. At 1.5.153–154, Malvolio
uses a similar image to describe how
Cesario straddles the border between
boy and man (*One would think his
mother's milk were scarce out of him*).
Both instances rely on a common
Renaissance notion of female
physiology as one governed by fluids
(blood, milk, and urine) and hence
unstable as compared to a male body.
Renaissance physiologists used the
term "the mother" to describe the
anatomical phenomenon of the
wandering womb, which was thought
to produce the symptoms of hysteria
in its travels throughout the female
body. Some of Shakespeare's male
characters use the image figuratively
to describe an unmanly propensity
to emotion. In this vein, Viola speaks
in 2.2 of the frailty of women's waxen
hearts, a speech which tallies with
Sebastian's understanding of female
vulnerability. However, a discourse
of female stoicism is also present
in the play, in Viola's own image of
*patience on a monument, / Smiling at
grief* (2.4.113–114); in the image of the
Roman matron Lucrece on Olivia's
signet ring (2.5.89); in Sir Toby's
reference to the biblical Susannah in
2.3.73–74; and in his ironic reference
to the diminutive Maria as Penthesilea, Queen of the Amazons, a tribe

of female warriors (2.3.164).

Page 113
2.3.9   *four elements*

The four elements of matter
corresponded to the four humors
and their respective fluids (choler,
blood, phlegm, and bile), which in
Galenic physiology were thought to
compose the human body. Differences among personality and moral
types were thought to result from
imbalances among these fluids, as
were genders—women, for instance,
were considered phlegmatic, or
cooler than men. Good health, on
the other hand, was understood to
be achieved through the calibra-
tion of their balance, accomplished
through purging, bleeding, feasting,
or fasting. The play is in a sense above
such processes of correction. For
instance, both Orsino's love-melan-
choly and Olivia's self-indulgent
mourning must be restrained and
counterbalanced in order for comic
and social harmony to be achieved.
The imagery of humors abounds in
the play, and has even led some critics
to hazard in Maria's *M.O.A.I.* (2.5.106)
a reference to the four elements:
Mare, Orbis, Aer, Ignus.

Page 125
2.3.129   *sometimes he is kind of puritan*

The puritan faction in Parliament, in
fact, succeeded in engineering the
ordered closing of the theaters in
1642. Puritans were in turn mocked
for their preening self-confidence
in their own spiritual status as the

chosen of God, whose salvation was secure and hence evident in their exemplary conduct. While their antipathy to certain kinds of social disorder was not out of keeping with the Tudor-Stuart ideological emphasis on hierarchy, puritans' self-righteousness regarding their own ethical standing may have been a more disruptive social force than the activities they condemned. As Sir Toby's question at line 131 reveals, it is not exactly clear (as usual) what Sir Andrew specifically understands by the term, but both Malvolio's hostility to what he considers unruly behavior as well as his certainty of his own specialness qualify him for Maria's epithet. Note, however, that Maria, who can imitate her lady's handwriting, is not herself unacquainted with social ambition, and her intuition about Malvolio's delusions of grandeur may stem from the fact that it takes one to know one.

PAGE 271

5.1.236   *My father had a mole upon his brow*

The details of this recognition scene seemingly hamper its emotional effectiveness. A parental mole seems rather beside the point of the evidence provided by what has been asserted elsewhere (5.1.210 and 2.1.22) as the uncanny physical resemblance of the siblings and the coincidence of mutual shipwreck. There is furthermore something distracting about the repeti-

tion of Viola's age at her father's death, and, given the insistence on reciprocity, we are expecting a mention of Sebastian's age in turn. This exchange has led some readers to have wondered whether Shakespeare has forgotten that Sebastian and Viola are twins. On the other hand, the elaborate ritual could speak to the force of clothing in determining identity: Viola, when dressed as a boy, is seemingly unrecognizable as her former self.

PAGE 271

5.1.254   *But nature to her bias drew in that*

Here, Sebastian argues—somewhat to the contrary of the metaphor—that nature has saved Olivia from her mistaken attraction to a female mate. But the tension within the metaphor emerges from the fact that during the Renaissance, the tendency of nature was believed to be of like to like: the natural bias inside Olivia would cause her to roll toward the similarly female Viola. Likewise, Orsino chooses Cesario as an emissary to Olivia because his very lack of adult masculinity makes him more like Olivia, and thus the more congenial ambassador. Hence, the line also suggests that Olivia's mistake stemmed from the tendency in nature of like seeking like—in other words, the phrase means "nature, according to her bias, caused the mistake," a situation corrected by Sebastian's arrival.

Twelfe Night, Or what you will.

Actus Primus, Scæna Prima.

Enter Orsino Duke of Illyria, Curio, and other Lords.

Duke.

IF Musicke be the food of Loue, play on,
Giue me excesse of it : that surfetting,
The appetite may sicken, and so dye.
That straine agen, it had a dying fall :
O, it came ore my eare, like the sweet sound
That breathes vpon a banke of Violets ;
Stealing, and giuing Odour. Enough, no more,
Tis not so sweet now, as it was before.
O spirit of Loue, how quicke and fresh art thou,
That notwithstanding thy capacitie,
Receiueth as the Sea. Nought enters there,
Of what validity, and pitch so ere,
But falles into abatement, and low price
Euen in a minute ; so full of shapes is fancie,
That it alone, is high fantasticall.

Cu. Will you go go hunt my Lord?
Du. What *Curio*?
Cu. The Hart.
Du. Why so I do, the Noblest that I haue :
O when mine eyes did see *Oliuia* first,
Me thought she purg'd the ayre of pestilence ;
That instant was I turn'd into a Hart,
And my desires like fell and cruell hounds,
Ere since pursue me. How now what newes from her ?

Enter Valentine.

Val. So please my Lord, I might not be admitted,
But from her handmaid do returne this answer :
The Element it selfe, till seuen yeares heate,
Shall not behold her face at ample view :
But like a Cloystresse she will vailed walke,
And water once a day her Chamber round
With eye-offending brine : all this to season
A brothers dead loue, which she would keepe fresh
And lasting, in her sad remembrance.

Du. O she that hath a heart of that fine frame
To pay this debt of loue but to a brother,
How will she loue, when the rich golden shaft
Hath kill'd the flocke of all affections else
That liue in her. When Liuer, Braine, and Heart,
These soueraigne thrones, are all supply'd and fill'd
Her sweete perfections with one selfe king :
Away before me, to sweet beds of Flowres,
Loue-thoughts lye rich, when canopy'd with bowres.
Exeunt

Scena Secunda.

Enter Viola, a Captaine, and Saylors.

Vio. What Country (Friends) is this ?
Cap. This is Illyria Ladie.
Vio. And what should I do in Illyria?
My brother he is in Elizium,
Perchance he is not drown'd : What thinke you saylors ?
Cap. It is perchance that you your selfe were saued.
Vio. O my poore brother, and so perchance may he be.
Cap. True Madam, and to comfort you with chance,
Assure your selfe, after our ship did split,
When you, and those poore number saued with you,
Hung on our driuing boate : I saw your brother
Most prouident in perill, binde himselfe,
(Courage and hope both teaching him the practise)
To a strong Maste, that liu'd vpon the sea :
Where like *Orion* on the Dolphines backe,
I saw him hold acquaintance with the waues,
So long as I could see.

Vio. For saying so, there's Gold :
Mine owne escape vnfoldeth to my hope,
Whereto thy speech serues for authoritie
The like of him. Know'st thou this Countrey ?
Cap. I Madam well, for I was bred and borne
Not three houres trauaile from this very place.
Vio. Who gouernes heere ?
Cap. A noble Duke in nature, as in name.
Vio. What is his name?
Cap. Orsino.
Vio. Orsino : I haue heard my father name him.
He was a Batchellor then.
Cap. And so is now, or was so very late :
For but a month ago I went from hence,
And then 'twas fresh in murmure (as you know
What great ones do, the lesse will prattle of,)
That he did seeke the loue of faire *Oliuia*.
Vio. What's shee ?
Cap. A vertuous maid, the daughter of a Count
That dide some tweluemonth since, then leauing her
In the protection of his sonne, her brother,
Who shortly also dide : for whose deere loue
(They say) she hath abiur'd the sight
And company of men.
Vio. O that I seru'd that Lady,
And might not be deliuered to the world

Y 2   Till

Editing *Twelfth Night*
by David Scott Kastan

The earliest text of *Twelfth Night* is that which was published in the Folio of 1623, though the play was probably written sometime in 1601. It appears in the Folio as the thirteenth of the fourteen comedies that make up the first section of the volume, printed between *All's Well That Ends Well* and *The Winter's Tale*. It is an accurately printed text, likely derived either from the acting company's prompt copy or a scribal transcript of it (rather than from an authorial manuscript). One piece of evidence that the underlying manuscript derived from the theater is that actors' entrances are usually placed at the point at which they must enter the stage instead of where the other characters become aware of them, and exits, where obvious from the lines, are often unmarked.

In general the editorial work of this present edition is conservative, a matter of normalizing spelling, capitalization, and punctuation, removing superfluous italics, regularizing the names of characters, and rationalizing entrances and exits. A comparison of the edited text of 1.1.1–1.2.43 with the facsimile page of the Folio (see opposite) reveals some of the issues in this modernization. The speech prefixes are expanded and normalized for clarity, so that "Vio" becomes Viola, "Cu" becomes Curio, and the Folio's "Duke" (or "Du.")

is specified as Orsino. Spelling, capitalization, and italicization here regularly follow modern practices rather than the habits of the Folio's printers. As neither spelling nor punctuation in Shakespeare's time had yet been standardized, words were spelled in various ways that indicated their proximate pronunciation, and punctuation, which then was largely a rhythmical pointer rather than predominantly designed, as it is now, to clarify logical relations, was necessarily far more idiosyncratic than today. In any case, compositors were under no obligation to follow either the spelling or punctuation of their copy. Since the copy for *Twelfth Night* originated with a playhouse script, the spelling and punctuation of the Folio text is probably at several removes from Shakespeare's own hand; for most readers, then, there is little advantage in an edition that reproduces the spelling and punctuation of the Folio text. It does not accurately represent Shakespeare's writing habits, and it makes reading difficult in a way Shakespeare could never have anticipated or desired.

Therefore "Twelfe" in the title here becomes "Twelfth," while "fancie" in 1.1.14 becomes the familiar "fancy." In 1.2.36, "abiur'd" becomes "abjured," though it is interesting to note that "i" was then often used where we now use "j," just as "v" is used for our "u" in words like "vpon" in 1.1.6, and oppositely "u" is used for our "v," as in "haue" in 1.1.17. The intrusive "e's" in words like "Braine" (1.1.36) are eliminated, as is the "literary" capitalization of the noun. Although old spellings of words are consistently modernized, old forms of words (e.g., "wert," 1.5.25) are retained. The colon in 1.1.4 and the semicolon two lines later in the Folio respectively mark a heavy and a slightly less heavy pause rather than define a precise (and different) grammatical relation as they would in modern usage, and in this text they are replaced with punctuation that accords with modern practices. In all these cases, modernizing clarifies rather than alters Shakespeare's intentions. Thus, 1.1.1–8 reads in the Folio:

If Musicke be the food of Loue, play on,
Giue me excesse of it: that surfetting,
The appetite may sicken, and so dye.
That straine agen, it had a dying fall:
O, it came ore my eare, like the sweet sound
That breathes vpon a banke of Violets;
Stealing, and giuing Odour. Enough, no more,
'Tis not so sweet now, as it was before.

Modernized this reads:

If music be the food of love, play on.
Give me excess of it that, surfeiting,
The appetite may sicken and so die.
That strain again—it had a dying fall.
Oh, it came o'er my ear like the sweet sound
That breathes upon a bank of violets,
Stealing and giving odor. Enough, no more.
'Tis not so sweet now as it was before.

No doubt there is some loss in modernization. Clarity and consistency is admittedly gained at the expense of expressive detail, but normalizing spelling, capitalization, and punctuation allows the text to be read with far greater ease than the original, and essentially as it was intended to be understood. We trade the historical particulars of the text for clarity of meaning. If, inevitably, in such modernization we lose the historical feel of the play Shakespeare's contemporaries read, it is important to remember that Shakespeare's contemporaries would not have thought the Folio in any sense archaic or quaint, as these details inevitably make it for a reader today. The text would have seemed to them as modern as this one does to us. Indeed many of the Folio's

typographical peculiarities are the result of its effort to make the printed page look up to date for potential buyers.

Modern readers, however, cannot help but be distracted
by the different conventions they encounter on the Folio page. While
it is indeed of interest to see how orthography and typography have
changed over time, these changes are not primary concerns for most
readers of this edition. What little, then, is lost in a careful modernization of the text is more than made up for by the removal of the
artificial obstacle of unfamiliar spelling forms and punctuation
habits, which Shakespeare never could have intended as interpretive
difficulties for his readers.

Textual Notes

The list below records all substantive departures in this edition from the
Folio text of 1623. It does not record modernizations of spelling, nor-
malization in the use of capitals, corrections of obvious typographical
errors, adjustments of lineation, minor rewording or repositioning of
stage directions, or rationalizations of speech prefixes. The adopted
reading in this edition is given first in boldface and followed by the
original, rejected reading of the Folio, or noted as being absent from the
Folio text. Editorial stage directions are not collated but are enclosed
within brackets in the text. Latin stage directions are translated (e.g.,
"They all exit" for *Exeunt omnes*), and the Latin act and scene designation
of the Folio are similarly translated (e.g., Act One, scene one for *Actus
primus, scena prima*).

1.1.1SP **(and throughout) Orsino** Duke; **1.2.14 Arion**
Orion; **1.3.48SP Sir Andrew** Ma; **1.3.50 Mary Accost** Mary, accost;
1.3.55 Fare Far; **1.3.88 curl by** coole my; **1.3.89 me** we; **1.3.121 set**
sit; **1.3.124 That's** That ; **1.5.4SP (and throughout) Feste** not in F
(Clown or Clo.); **1.5.158SD Viola** Violenta; **1.5.284 County's** Countes;
2.2.30 our O; **2.2.31 made of** made, if; **2.3.2 *diluculo*** Deliculo;
2.3.24 leman Lemon; **2.3.125 a nayword** an ayword; **2.3.137 swaths**

swarths; **2.4.50SP Feste** not in F; **2.4.52 Fly . . . fly** Fye . . . fie;
2.4.54 yew Ew; **2.4.87 I** it; **2.5. 109 staniel** stallion; **2.5.136 born**
become; **2.5.136 achieve** atcheeues; **2.5.167 dear** deero; **2.5.185**
aqua-vitae Aqua vite; **3.1.7 king** Kings; **3.1.64 wise men** wisemens;
3.1.67 *vous* vou; **3.2.7 thee** the; **3.3.15 thanks—and** not in F; **3.4.23SP**
Olivia Mal; **3.4.66 tang** langer; **3.4.161 You** Yon; **3.4.206 thee**
the; **3.4.230–231 competent** computent; **4.2.5 in** in in; **4.2.37**
clerestories cleere stores; **4.2.49 haply** happily; **4.2.67 sport to**
sport; **4.3.1SP Sebastian** not in F; **5.1.195 pavin** panyn; **5.1.379 tiny**
tine; **5.1.384, 388, 392 With hey, ho, the wind and the rain** *with hey ho,*
etc.; **5.1.386, 390, 394 For the rain it raineth every day** *for the raine, etc.*

Twelfth Night on the Early Stage
by Claire McEachern

T he earliest mention of a performance of *Twelfth Night* records a staging in the banqueting hall of the Middle Temple, one of London's training schools for lawyers. The lawyer John Manningham noted the following in his diary entry for 2 February 1602, the feast of Candlemas:

At our feast wee had a play called 'Twelve night, or What You Will', much like the Commedy of Errors, or Menechmi in Plautus, but most like and neere to that in Italian called Ingnanni. A good practice in it to make the Steward believe his Lady Widdow was in love with him, by counterfeiting a letter as from his Lady in generall terms, telling him what she liked best in him, and prescribing his gesture in smiling, his aparaile, &c, and then when he came to practise making him believe they tooke him to be mad.[1]

From this document and others we know that this play, set in two noble households, was appropriately enough suited to performance in the space of the Tudor-Stuart banqueting hall; it was also performed at court at Easter 1618 and Candlemas 1623. Banquet halls were large rooms with a carved wooden screen at one end (in modern

Fig 1. In the large London playhouses, the balcony above the stage could be used for staging, seating, or to house musicians.

Fig 2. English Renaissance drama made minimal use of sets or backdrops. In the absence of a set, the stage pillars could be incorporated into the action, standing in for trees and other architectural elements.

Fig 3. *The discovery space, located in the middle of the backstage wall, could be used as a third entrance as well as a location for scenes requiring special staging, such as in a tomb or bedchamber.*

Fig 4. *A trapdoor led to the area below the stage, known as "Hell" (as contrasted with the painted ceiling, known as "Heaven" or the "heavens"). Ghosts or other supernatural figures could descend through the trap, and it could also serve as a grave.*

parlance, more like a substantial half wall), often crowned with a gallery for musicians. The screen had at least two doors separated by a space of at least a door's width, which served as a means of access to and separation from the kitchens and servants' workspace. Along with inn yards, such halls were sites of the preprofessional English theater, and theater historians conjecture that they served as models for the configuration of the playing space in the later public theaters. *Twelfth Night* probably had its first performance in the Globe Theatre, but in its performances in the feasting rooms of the Middle Temple or the court the play was, in some sense, coming home.

From contemporary sketches and descriptions we know that the public theaters utilized thrust stages, platforms measuring as much as forty feet across and extending out from one side to the middle of the yard. These theaters were enclosed, round or polygonal buildings whose walls contained seating galleries; patrons could also pay to stand around three sides of the stage platform. At the rear of the stage was a tiring-house, or players' changing room, with at least two doors opening onto the stage and ample enough so that properties as large as a bed could be brought on or off. Above the tiring-house was another gallery, providing on- or above-stage seats for theater-goers but also a supplemental playing space and possible location for musicians. The stage was roofed, with two supporting pillars located downstage. This roof in turn had a smaller roofed structure atop it, from which stagehands could lower equipment; the stage platform itself also contained a trapdoor through which properties and persons could rise. The playhouse was probably elaborately carved, painted, and decorated. Curtains might cover the tiring-house doors, or be hung just behind their openings so as to shield their interior from view when the doors were open. Curtains may have also covered the tiring-house façade between the doors, which may have been recessed, thus providing a possible discovery space.

The public theater was thus a technologically more sophisticated space than the banqueting house, but resembled its antecedent in its essential simplicity—two doors opening onto a playing area. As its portability to the Middle Temple indicates, *Twelfth Night* is not a play that requires any more than this simplicity. The play's locations are the interiors of Orsino's court (1.1, 1.4, 2.4) and Olivia's house (1.3, 1.5, 2.3); Olivia's garden or orchard, for the box tree scene (2.5) and the duel between Sir Andrew and Cesario (3.4); perhaps another exterior locale of Olivia's house (3.1, 4.1, 4.3, 5.1); and the location of the dark house (4.2), presumably somewhere within Olivia's house. Places indicated offstage but not represented are the "cubiculo" (3.2.47) in which Sir Andrew will compose his challenge to Cesario and the "chantry by" (4.3) into which Olivia ushers Sebastian in order to plight her troth. Between these two households lies an indeterminate outdoor space or street, where Viola speaks to her sea captain and Antonio with Sebastian (1.2, 2.1, 2.2, 3.3).

It does not pay, however, to be too niggling in determining these locations; Olivia's orchard, for instance, is perhaps the same thing as her garden, and though we are tempted to imagine the orchard as a private space, it is public enough that Antonio can stumble across the duel between Cesario and Sir Andrew, and that the officers can then stumble across Antonio. The main thing to be aware of is whose household we are in, and the majority of the action takes place in Olivia's and its environs. Language usually gives us our necessary bearings: his house or hers, indoors or out?

The use of the two tiring-house doors for entrances and exits were governed by a set of established conventions. Characters generally exited a space/room through the door they entered, unless the dialogue indicates a transit (e.g., 1.2.60: "Lead me on.") Once a group of actors exits, the next group will enter through the other door. Finally, parting actors exit through separate doors, and when meeting onstage they enter through "several" or separate doors, as Viola and

Malvolio do at 2.2.[2] A scene is continuous until the stage is cleared (although see the note on 3.4.256), but a new scene does not necessarily
imply a new location, as a different set of persons could come into the
same imaginary space.

Unlike some farces involving twins, not much depends
in this play upon near misses of the twins themselves. In fact, it is
possible to imagine the same actor doubling the parts up until the
final scene.[3] There is however some potential for confusion on the
parts of both the audience and characters, for instance, in the se-
quence of 1.5, 2.1, and 2.2: Cesario leaves Olivia in 1.5, and Malvolio is
sent in pursuit of her; in the next scene Antonio and Sebastian enter
for the first time; then in the next scene, Malvolio and Viola enter "at
several doors." When Antonio and Sebastian enter—presumably not
through the door through which Malvolio and Cesario have exited—
the audience may do a double take until Sebastian reveals his identity
(which he does quickly). Although Sebastian moves to part, Antonio
probably follows him out through the same door, probably not the
one through which they entered. Then, in the next scene, Cesario
and Malvolio enter through separate doors, meaning that Cesario
must either enter through the door through which Sebastian has just
exited, or that Malvolio must. If Malvolio does, and thus crosses paths
with Sebastian (even in an imaginary offstage locale), his question,
"Were not *you* even now with the Countess Olivia?" (emphasis mine),
could indicate a more than usual degree of peevishness: he sees
Cesario coming through one door, but has just passed him, perhaps
attempted to address him, in another. In the Elizabethan theater,
the fact that boy actors took the roles of women meant that the
visual resemblance of Cesario and Sebastian might in fact have been
more convincing than in some modern productions, where casting
choices must either seek to minimize the physical difference between
these performers or brazenly refuse to do so. If the resemblance is
hard to discern, the audience may be in the same position of slight

bewilderment. Cesario makes a point of mentioning the "moderate pace" with which he has traveled from Olivia's household, which is funnier if Sebastian's pace is not moderate and Malvolio is out of breath from chasing the wrong twin, or wondering how he could be in two places so speedily.

Scholars believe that original productions were fast paced so as to sustain the attention of a daylit audience with many things to look at besides the onstage action, and, since there was no scenery on the Elizabethan stage apart from that provided in the language, the clearing of the stage alone often indicated a scene change. There are records of some props, often quite large: the theater impresario Philip Henslowe included on his list of properties, for instance, three trees: "1 baye tree," "1 tree of gowlden apelles, Tantelouse tre,"[4] which suggests that an actual box tree could have been trundled on and off for the scenes in Olivia's garden (or, as in the play *A Warning for Fair Women*, hoisted up through the trapdoor). However, it would have been just as convincing and more efficient on the Globe stage for a downstage pillar to have served as a putative tree, or as the cover of the orchard in which Sir Andrew reluctantly cowers in wait for Viola to enter in Act Three, scene four. The basic requirement of both scenes is that the audience be able to see and hear all parties to a scene, even while believing that they could not necessarily see each other.

The dark house scene of Act Four, scene two is an unusually differentiated location within Olivia's household; it could easily have been played with Malvolio behind a curtain of one of the tiring-house screen doors, or behind a curtain between the doors. The only requirement is that Malvolio be audible to the audience but incapable of seeing Feste/Sir Topas. The trapdoor covered by a grate is another possibility but may risk both the fictions of Feste's invisibility and Malvolio's darkness. Modern productions that seek to emphasize the penal quality of Malvolio's suffering have tended toward this kind of choice.

1. John Manningham, Diary, quoted in Geoffrey Bullough, *Narrative and Dramatic Sources of Shakespeare II: The Comedies, 1597–1603*, 1958, 269.

2. The guidelines are those of T. J. King, who provides a possible sketch of the Middle Temple staging of *Twelfth Night in his Shakespearean Staging, 1599–1642* (Cambridge, MA, 1971), 99–115. See also Tim Fitzpatrick, "Stage management, dramaturgy, and spatial semiotics in Shakespeare's dialogue," *Theatre Research International* 23 1 (1999): 1–23.

3. T. J. King conjectures that eight actors can play nine principal male roles, and three boys play three principal female roles; seven men can play six small speaking parts and five mutes; three boys play three mute attendants on Olivia. *Casting Shakespeare's Plays, 1590–1642* (Cambridge, MA, 1992), 88.

4. In Andrew Gurr, *The Shakespearean Stage, 1574–1642* (Cambridge, MA 1980), 171–172.

Significant Performances

1602   Middle Temple (also at court, Easter 1618 and Candelmas 1623).

1661, 1662, 1669   Restoration revivals seen by an unimpressed Samuel Pepys at the Duke's Theatre, who records in his diary: "a silly play, and not at all related to the name or day." *Twelfth Night* formed part of the repertoire of William Davenant, who along with James Killiegrew had one of two patents on theater production in this period.

1703   Adaptation of Charles Burnaby, *Love Betrayed, or the Agreeable Disappointment*. The Theatre, Lincoln's Inn Fields. A typical eighteenth-century rewrite of the play (retaining only fifty-eight lines of Shakespeare's original poetry) that merged the characters of Malvolio and Sir Andrew to create a composite jealous seeker of Olivia's favor who duels with Cesario. On the other hand, it divided the character of Maria into two: an aged companion for Sir Toby, and a young confidant for Olivia, "and the two halves by no means equal the whole."[1] This latter innovation was perhaps a measure to multiply the roles available for female actors, who had not been allowed onto the English stage during Shakespeare's time. Malvolio's plot became central, as it had been to Manningham's account (see "*Twelfth Night* on the Early Stage") as well as to the 1640 mention of *Twelfth Night* by Leonard

Digges, who in a discussion of Shakespeare's popularity that prefaced an edition of the poems wrote, "lo, in a trice / The cockpit galleries, boxes all are full / to hear Malvolio, that cross-gartered gull."

1740–1741   Drury Lane, Shakespeare's text revived, although throughout the eighteenth and nineteenth centuries it would be considered a vehicle for musical effects and the star power of individual actresses such as Dorothea Jordan, Sarah Siddons, and Helen Faucit; these actresses' musical talents were often displayed at the expense of the actor playing Feste. Bell's acting editions of Shakespeare (1773–75, 1778) cut both "O mistress mine" and "Come away, come away, death" and their surrounding context, leaving the clown to sing only in lighter keys. Feste's concluding song, "When that I was and a little tiny boy" was restored only in 1799.

1820   An operatic version by Frederick Reynolds, an apotheosis of the musical emphasis, with songs and lyrics interpolated from the sonnets, *Two Gentlemen of Verona*, *Venus and Adonis*, and *Henry VIII* (in the first act alone). Act Four contained the masque of Juno and Ceres from *The Tempest*. Not only Viola but Olivia was enlisted as a singer. While critics were skeptical, they allowed that *Twelfth Night* made for a better candidate for this sort of treatment than Reynolds's other foray into Shakespeare, *The Comedy of Errors*.

1850   Charles Kean's production indoctrinated *Twelfth Night* into the nineteenth century's obsession with a hyperrealist verisimilitude in which the true star was the scenery. Kean's 1850 production ran forty times during the thirteen months of the Great Exposition of 1851, outpacing all other Shakespearean offerings. Similarly, in Henry Irving's otherwise unremarkable 1884 production set in Venice, "the art of landscape gardening, as pursued in Illyria three hundred years ago, appears to have reached a very high pitch of excellence."[2] Such treatment was to reach its apogee in the 1901 production of Herbert Beerbohm Tree, in which the garden of Olivia, for instance, unfurled "terrace by terrace to the extreme back of the stage, with very real grass, real fountains, paths and descending steps." Scenery of this epoch was often so cumbersome and time-consuming to change that it required, in addition to heavy cutting, the rearranging of the order of scenes, and the transposition of action from one scene to another, so as to make most efficient use of the spectacle. ("The disadvantage lay in the fact that, once put up, this scene . . . was perforce used for many of the Shakespearean episodes for which it was absurdly inappropriate.")[3]

1895 William Poel and his Elizabethan Stage Company inaugurated a backlash against the complexity of Victorian stage spectacle; his production of *Twelfth Night* was staged at the Middle Temple once again with no scenery apart from its elaborately carved screen and a chair and a table as the only props. The de-emphasis of the visual made it once again practical to speak all of Shakespeare's text, with only a ten-minute intermission. This production's choice of Elizabethan costuming would reappear frequently throughout the twentieth century.

1950–2000 The increased mobility made possible for women in the wake of the Second World War, as well as the influence of the sexual revolution of the 1960s, meant that productions of the latter half of the twentieth century often emphasize the boyish liberation in Viola's disguise, as well the homoerotic dynamic in the relations between Orsino and Cesario, Antonio and Sebastian, and Olivia and Cesario. The most resonant influence of the latter twentieth century, however, came from Peter Hall's **1958** Shakespeare Memorial Theatre production and its inauguration of a tradition of "autumnal" productions, featuring aging or unkempt Festes, an emphasis on melancholy, and an increased attention to the cruelty in Malvolio's punishment. Terry Hands's **1979** production of the Royal Shakespeare

Company, for instance, set the play in winter, and in John Caird's **1983** RSC production the stage was overpowered by a gigantic and somewhat menacing bare tree. The **1996** film of Trevor Nunn provides another melancholy reading, in which the heavy stone buildings and stormy weather of the Cornish coast set the tone.

1. George C. Odell, *Shakespeare from Betterton to Irving*, 2 vols, i, (New York, 1920), 82.

2. Odell, op. cit., vol. ii, 432.

3. Ibid., 455.

Inspired by *Twelfth Night*

Stage

Recent theatrical adaptations of *Twelfth Night* seem to take their cue from Duke Orsino's famous opening line, "If music be the food of love, play on"—nearly all adaptations from the last fifty years have been musicals. In 1968 a rock musical adaptation by Danny Apolinar, Hal Hester, and Donald Driver opened Off-Broadway. Called *Your Own Thing*, it refashioned the action of Shakespeare's play to center around the romantic entanglements of a rock band called The Apocalypse. *Twelfth Night*'s concerns with unrequited love, mistaken identities, and sexual ambiguity adapted readily to the manners and mores of the 1960s counterculture, and the show's authors saw in Shakespeare's subtitle, *What You Will*, a parallel with the mantra of that era's young people, "do your own thing." The show was one of the first successful rock musicals in theater history, opening the same year that *Hair*—another, more famous musical about 1960s youth culture—moved to Broadway.

In 1997, the musical *Play On!* transported the court of Illyria to "The Magical Kingdom of Harlem" in "the swinging '40s." Built around a score of jazz standards by the legendary bandleader, Duke Ellington, the show centers on a young songwriter named Vy who disguises herself as a man in order to break into the male-dominated music industry. In her new, masculine role as Vy-Man, Vy becomes the go-between for Duke, a bandleader trying to woo a chanteuse named Lady Liv. During his prolific career, Ellington wrote a number of pieces inspired by Shakespeare, though none specifically based on *Twelfth Night*. Part of the fun of *Play On!* lies in the unexpected ways in which classic songs made popular by Ellington—such as Billy Strayhorn's "Take the A Train"—are worked into the Shakespeare-inspired storyline.

Illyria, another musical version of *Twelfth Night*, opened at the Shakespeare Theatre of New Jersey in 2004 after a successful debut with the Prospect Theater Company in New York. Unlike *Your Own Thing* or *Play On!*, *Illyria* maintains the original Shakespearean characters and setting as well as much of the dialogue. Expanding on the prominence of music in Shakespeare's play, *Illyria* features a score of original musical numbers, including a comic patter song for Feste entitled "Silly Little Syllogisms" and a raucous drinking song for Sir Toby, "Cakes and Ale." The show proved highly successful for the Shakespeare Theatre, resulting in a cast recording in 2005.

Most recently, in 2005, the Broadway stage witnessed an unlikely partnership between the drama of William Shakespeare and the music of Elvis Presley. Responding to the current vogue for jukebox musicals—shows in which the songs of a particular pop star or group are collected to provide the score for an original story—*All Shook Up* told the story of a young girl named Natalie, living in a small American town in 1955, who falls in love with a pompadoured rebel named Chad. The tomboyish Natalie disguises herself as a man to get close to Chad, but she soon feels like checking into the Heartbreak Hotel when she learns that Chad loves another woman, the sexy museum curator, Miss Sandra. When Chad sends Natalie's alter ego, "Ed," to woo Miss Sandra, complications arise as Miss Sandra falls for the handsome young mechanic. *All Shook Up* closed after seven months on Broadway and has gone on to tour nationally.

Film & Television

In the Oscar-winning film *Shakespeare In Love* (1999), a young William Shakespeare falls in love with a noblewoman named Viola de Lesseps, and the resulting romance inspires him to write the greatest love story of all Western literature, *Romeo and Juliet*. Near the film's conclusion, Will and Viola's relationship is cut off abruptly when Viola is forced to marry a nobleman, Lord Wessex, and sail with him to his American plantation. Shakespeare, inspired by his grief, begins to conceive of a play about a young woman shipwrecked on a distant shore. Will names the character Viola, and thus the film ends with Shakespeare beginning to write what will become *Twelfth Night*.

A collaboration between HBO and an international team of animators and puppeteers led to the creation of *Shakespeare: The Animated Tales*, a series of half-hour animated versions of Shakespeare's plays. A team of English, Welsh, and Russian puppeteers worked on the episode based on *Twelfth Night* (1982). By casting the characters as puppets, the filmmakers hit upon a resonant metaphor for the ways in which love animates and manipulates people, causing them to behave in strange new ways. Due to the half-hour running time, the plot of *Twelfth Night* was cut and rearranged quite drastically for this production: Malvolio, Sir Andrew, and Sir Toby, are given short shrift and are completely left out of the final scene, which is a simple reunion of the twins with Orsino and Olivia.

A silent version of *Twelfth Night* was recently preserved and restored by the British Film Institute and is currently available on DVD as part of their *Silent Shakespeare* anthology. Made in the United States in 1910, this film was directed by Charles Kent, who appears in the film as Malvolio. A new piano score written especially for the restored film provides the musical accompaniment. In the earliest days of film production, many actors disdained the new medium, which they felt cheapened their art. Making film versions of Shakespeare's plays was one way to entice reluctant actors to appear in a film, as the

Bard lent an aura of class to the seemingly pedestrian, commercially oriented medium. This charming _Twelfth Night_ is valuable for the glimpse it provides of a nearly century-old acting style, which can seem rather bombastic and overdone to contemporary audiences yet often manages to achieve a simplicity and subtlety that feels very modern.

Not all filmmakers are interested in Shakespeare's plays as high art, as evidenced by Playboy Films's entry, _Playboy Twelfth Night_ (1972). Produced by Hugh Hefner, it was the only film version of the play to be made, apart from TV versions, between the 1910 American silent and Trevor Nunn's 1996 version. The film makes full use of the play's erotic potential, letting the play's gender confusions and romantic entanglements serve as the prelude to a variety of sexual scenarios.

In 2006's comedy _She's the Man_, the city of Illyria becomes the American boarding school Illyria Prep. When her girls' team is cut and she's refused admission onto the boy's team, teen soccer phenom Viola Johnson does the next best thing: she disguises herself as her brother Sebastian and enrolls in his place at her former rival school (Sebastian having conveniently absconded to London to pursue his music career). At Illyria Prep, Viola develops a crush on her handsome, team captain roommate Duke, who is in turn in love with the beautiful Olivia, who is, naturally, in love herself with the sensitive Sebastian. Things get even more complicated when Olivia's nerdy admirer, Malcolm, decides to start snooping around in "Sebastian's" past . . . and the real Sebastian decides to return early from Europe.

Literature

Thirteenth Night, Alan R. Gordon's 1999 mystery novel, fashions itself as a sequel to Shakespeare's play. In the novel, we find that Olivia's fool Feste is not exactly the man Shakespeare portrayed him to be. Feste is really Theophilos, a member of the powerful thirteenth-century Fool's Guild, a semisecret organization of jesters and clowns who perform covert acts of espionage and undertake high-security political operations. (In fact, it is revealed that the Fool's Guild orchestrated the original shipwreck that brought Viola and Sebastian to Illyria.) Fifteen years after the events of *Twelfth Night*, Feste receives word that Duke Orsino has been killed. Feste suspects that the disgruntled Malvolio has finally made good on his vow to be revenged, so he returns to Illyria to investigate the murder. Since *Thirteenth Night*, Gordon has written three more mysteries featuring Feste: *Jester Leaps In* (2000), *A Death in the Venetian Quarter* (2002), and *Widow of Jerusalem* (2003).

Another sequel to *Twelfth Night*—as well as a more sympathetic portrayal of Malvolio—can be found in Gabriel Josipovici's short story "A Changeable Report" (1982). In it, Malvolio narrates the events of his life following those depicted in *Twelfth Night*, as well as his anguish at his abusive treatment and his desire to enact revenge against his abusers. Malvolio's various revenge fantasies borrow scenarios from *Othello* and *The Tempest*, and he is plagued with dreams and images that readers may recognize from *Macbeth*, *Cymbeline*, *King Lear*, and *The Merchant of Venice*. Feste's songs haunt Malvolio most of all. Malvolio ends the story as a broken man but is determined to go on with his life, realizing that perhaps his ability to survive in the face of torment is the best revenge of all.

For Further Reading
by Claire McEachern

Astington, John. "Malvolio and the Eunuchs: Text and Revels in *Twelfth Night*." *Shakespeare Survey* 46 (1992): 23–34. This article discusses the biblical source of Malvolio's speech on greatness and goes on to consider the role of festival and the ritual punishment of sexual license in early modern notions of community.

Barber, C. L. "Testing Courtesy and Humanity in *Twelfth Night*." *Shakespeare's Festive Comedy*. Princeton: Princeton University Press, 1959. Barber relates the play's theme and movements to Saturnalian rituals of feasting, finding in the play's many inversions of gender and status a liberating effect for characters and audience alike.

Bullough, Geoffrey. *Narrative and Dramatic Sources of Shakespeare II: The Comedies, 1597–1603*. New York: Columbia University Press, 1958. Bullough sketches Shakespeare's possible debt to a variety of sources in which a twin girl pursues her love in disguise (*Gl'Ingannati* [1537], Matthew Bandello's *Novelle* [1554], and Barnaby Riche's story of "Apolonius and Silla" in *Riches Farewell to Militarie Profession*). He also notes what Shakespeare did not find in these places. The sources are then reprinted and translated.

Carnegie, David. "'Malvolio Within': Performance Perspectives on the Dark House." *Shakespeare Quarterly* 52, no. 3 (2001): 393–414. Carnegie provides an illuminating historical survey of different stagings of the dark house scene, as they have changed in response to cultural moment, theatrical technology, and conceptions of madness. He concludes with speculations on how the scene could have been played on an Elizabethan stage.

Duffin, Ross W. *Shakespeare's Songbook*. New York: W. W. Norton, 2005. A handsomely produced and illustrated volume that prints settings and lyrics and conjectures links between different plays' uses of song. Comes with a CD recording of many of the songs.

Elam, Keir. "The Fertile Eunuch: *Twelfth Night*, Early Modern Intercourse, and the Fruits of Castration." *Shakespeare Quarterly* 47, no. 1 (1996): 1–36. An essay that uses Viola's intention to disguise herself as a eunuch as a point of departure into an inquiry into the play's relation to its classical sources, Renaissance notions of gender difference, and early modern civilizing processes.

Everett, Barbara. "Or What You Will." *Essays in Criticism* 35, no. 4 (1985): 294–314. Everett's measure of the play's moral seriousness examines the presence of time, musical harmonies both literal and metaphoric, and the stylistic elusiveness peculiar to its language.

Greenblatt, Stephen. "Fiction and Friction." *Shakespearean Negotiations* Oxford: Clarendon, 1988. A wide-ranging and influential essay that reads the play in the contexts of early modern understandings of gender difference.

Hollander, John. "*Twelfth Night* and the Morality of Indulgence." *Sewanee Review* 67 (1959): 220–338. Reprinted in *Essays in Shakespearean Criticism*, edited by James L. Calderwood and Harold E. Toliver. Englewood Cliffs, NJ: Prentice-Hall, 1970. Hollander finds Shakespeare's play to be a direct contrast to Ben Jonson's comedy of humors, arguing that the play depicts a process of emotional and moral catharsis where balance and health are achieved through the overindulgence and satiety of intemperate appetites.

Howard, Jean E. "The Orchestration of *Twelfth Night*: The Rhythm of Restraint and Release." *Shakespeare's Art of Orchestration: Stage Technique and Audience Response.* Urbana and Chicago: University of Illinois Press, 1984. Howard examines how Shakespeare's methods help to shape and control the response of an audience and their relation to comic convention.

Peguiney, Joseph. "The Two Antonios and Same-Sex Love in *Twelfth Night* and *The Merchant of Venice*." *English Literary Renaissance* 22, no. 2 (1992): 201–21. Through an examination of diction, character, and structure, Peguiney makes a solid case for the explicit and reciprocally homo-erotic nature of the relationship between Antonio and Sebastian, as well as tracing the evidence of bisexual desire elsewhere in the play.

Seng, Peter. *Vocal Songs in the Plays of Shakespeare: A Critical History.* Cambridge, MA: Harvard University Press, 1967. The standard hand-book detailing the songs, their provenances, possible settings, and critical estimates.

Smith, Bruce, ed. *Twelfth Night: Texts and Contexts.* Boston: Bedford/St. Martin's, 2001. A hefty and diverse sampling of contemporary documents representing some of the contexts that inform many of the play's identities: romance, music, disguise, household, puri-tans, and clowns.

Taylor, A.B. "Shakespeare Rewriting Ovid: Olivia's Interview with Viola
    and the Narcissus Myth." *Shakespeare Survey* 50 (2002): 81–89. Taylor's
    close reading of Shakespeare's Ovidian source sheds light on the
    play's concerns with twinship, false images, and self-knowledge.

Yachnin, Paul. "Reversal of Fortune: Shakespeare, Middleton, and the
    Puritans." *English Literary History 700* (2003): 757–86. Yachnin examines
    how the character of Malvolio, as a low-born servant dependent
    upon an aristocratic hierarchy for advancement, serves as a figure
    for the professional players themselves.